I0087112

THE WAY OF THE GOOD HEDONIST

D D WORDEN

Edge of the World Press

Copyright © 2013 by D D Worden

All rights reserved.

Published by Edge of the World Press

Contact - edgeoftheworldpress@gmail.com

ISBN-13: 978-0615838540

ISBN-10: 0615838545

I'd like to thank Erin, who told me to write this book, not knowing I'd already started. Some might call it a coincidence but I do not.

CONTENTS

CONTENTS

CONTENTS

INTRODUCTION

The title of this book is a nod to "The Way Of Zen" by Alan Watts, which I read when I was eighteen, around forty years ago. It was my first step on a path that eventually led here, to writing this book. Of course I'm no Allan Watts, so comparisons end at the title. I wouldn't even want to be him, because he was an alcoholic. When I first learned that fact I was shocked, but soon loved how it humanized him. With such a brilliant mind and vast knowledge he was still flawed and vulnerable like the rest of us; which points to the fact we aren't just our minds, we are experiencing, feeling, emotional creatures. One can be brilliant and yet behave like an idiot, because we act primarily out of feeling, and our feelings can be stupid even if the mind isn't. Fortunately it's possible to make them less stupid once we understand they are more central to our functioning than our minds. Feeling is the ground we stand on, and the drive toward pleasure and away from suffering is what steers us. It's a fact so basic and ever-present it can disappear into the background.

1

DEFINITION

Hedonism, as described in my dictionary, is:

1. The ethical doctrine that pleasure, variously conceived of in terms of happiness of the individual or of society, is the principal good and the proper aim of action.

2. The theory that a person always acts in such a way as to seek pleasure and avoid pain.

3. The self-indulgent pursuit of pleasure as a way of life.

For the purposes of this book the second definition is mainly what I mean by "hedonism". I see it as an evident fact of life, not an ethical doctrine or lifestyle choice. You don't choose to be a hedonist any more than you chose to be born in the first place. This is an important point. It means I'm not telling anyone to be hedonistic or a hedonist, or self-indulgent, but rather just to see the truth of their own self and reality. Please keep this in mind.

2

WE ARE ALL HEDONISTS

Seeking pleasure and avoiding suffering is the basic engine that drives and animates us all. This is why I say we are all hedonists. Not that we choose to be but that we are born as such and remain so until the grave. Deny it all you'd like, it won't change the facts. From first breath to last, you will be a hedonist.

This isn't a bad thing, it's a necessary thing. Without it we couldn't exist. Would we eat if eating wasn't pleasurable and hunger unpleasant? Would we breed? Would we get up out of bed? Would we do anything if there weren't rewards of pleasure and punishments of pain? Isn't this the mechanism at our core that prods us to action? What would we be without it? What would motivate us?

Perhaps you think, "I'm certainly not a hedonist! I prove it every day I drag myself to work! There's no pleasure in that!" But don't you go to your job to earn money to use in an effort to avoid suffering and increase pleasure? Isn't being poor, hungry and homeless seen as being worse suffering with less potential pleasure than working a job you may hate? Though you are accepting a certain amount of discomfort and suffering, your motivation and goal in doing so is to secure a certain amount of pleasure and avoid worse discomfort and suffering. Being a hedonist doesn't mean you can't be practical or strategic and plan ahead, just that your principal motivation is pleasure in some way or another.

Someone with a masochistic or self-punishment proclivity might appear to contradict what I'm saying, but however it may appear on the surface, the pain they inflict on themselves is part of a psychological scheme that's desperately trying to remove or mask some particular suffering in themselves to reach a state that's less painful and more pleasurable. Using pain to remove or mask a greater pain may be a crude strategy but it still serves the basic hedonistic drive.

Perhaps you are a person who selflessly helps others and is very modest in your indulgences. How could you be a hedonist? Well, why do you help others? Does it give you joy? Alleviate guilt? Make you feel good about yourself? Is it what you think God wants you to do? Is it what your compassion, empathy, love or sense of duty dictate? All of these either avoid suffering or lead to pleasure in one way or another, directly or indirectly.

There's just no way around it. All our actions are in some way about seeking pleasure or avoiding suffering. Even when acting purely out of compassion or empathy for others. Although it's coming from an unselfish place, having compassion or empathy means you personally feel someone else's pain, so helping them helps remove that pain from yourself and you feel better. So though it may appear completely unselfish there still is a self-directed component involving a decrease in suffering and increase in pleasure for oneself.

What if you believe you're doing it for God? Then ask yourself why. Why do you want to please God?

I see four possibilities: You want to out of fear, respect, love, or for favor.

Fear is about avoiding suffering. Pleasing one you love or respect is pleasurable, and displeasing them is painful. And doing something to gain favor is obviously about hope of receiving pleasure or avoiding suffering.

No matter how selflessly one may believe they're "serving God", there is always a self-serving pleasure/pain angle lurking somewhere within it; be it blatantly crude or of the most subtle and sublime, it's there.

THE MOST SELFLESS ACT

How about when someone impulsively risks their life to rescue a stranger? Surely there can't be any hint of hedonism in that?! Right?

It may seem an exception because they risk their own safety and are acting with utter selflessness, but isn't the rescuer still acting out of an aversion to suffering? Not their own suffering but that of another? In that moment the suffering of another seems to override the danger to themselves and they act. It doesn't prove they aren't hedonists, it proves they are capable of great empathy, selflessness and bravery, and that their aversion to suffering can extend beyond their borders to a stranger to such a degree that they will risk their own life on impulse, much like if the stranger were their own limb. That supremely selfless instinct of the moment may reveal our true nature as being much more than just the little selfish egos we so often appear to be. But even when completely selfless, our motivations are still rooted in an attraction to pleasure and an aversion to suffering. It's fundamental.

Look closely and honestly and you'll see how all motivation, from sinner to saint, can be broken down to seeking, maintaining, or increasing pleasure, and avoiding, limiting, or escaping suffering. Though there are vast differences in the various forms of pleasure sought or pain avoided, and in the methods used to do so, all motivation is about our basic and fundamental attraction to pleasure and repulsion to suffering. At our core, everyone is a hedonist. This fact doesn't insult or belittle us, it unites us all, for seeing this truth about ourselves removes a level of self-deception and illusion which divides us from others and alienates us from our true selves and the greater reality we exist in. Some will protest and resist any such notion because it seems to make them less than what they fancy themselves to be. This is just a basic suffering avoidance tactic, denial. Their prejudiced, simplistic, and negative view of hedonism keeps them from ever embracing their own truth.

The good hedonist embraces the truth.

3

BAD REPUTATION
THE IGNORANT, INCOMPETENT OR IMPOTENT

Hedonism has a bad reputation. It's often seen as being shallow, self-indulgent, selfish, impulsive, immoral, lacking in virtue, and sometimes reckless or self-destructive. The main reason for this is because of an association of hedonism with only the base physical/sensual pleasures (sex being chief) and intoxication with drink, drugs or whatever (sex, drugs and rock & roll!), but there's no valid reason to limit hedonism to just the pursuit of those sorts of pleasures. In fact, it's ridiculous. Love is arguably a greater pleasure, so why isn't hedonism associated with that? Why not with states of profound religious or spiritual ecstasy? Why not with the wholesome joys of parenthood, or a child's joy at play? Why limit it? Shouldn't all pleasure be included; especially the greatest, deepest and most fulfilling pleasures? Obviously any hedonist worth their salt should be pursuing those with the most vigor and attention. It seems to me only ignorant, incompetent, or impotent hedonists would not.

With the full spectrum of pleasure included and embraced, the perception of hedonism as being shallow, self-centered and immoral must go out the window.

After all, doesn't love - a pleasure - inspire the greatest selflessness, morality, and depth us humans are capable of?

It's blindness and ignorance to see hedonism as only associated with our impulsive animal nature and base physical/sensual indulgences, when in truth pleasure is intimately connected to so much more, stretching far beyond. Hedonism isn't a closed circular track always leading back onto itself; it's an open highway that ultimately leads to our flowering and the pinnacle of what we can be.

The good hedonist's embrace of pleasure stretches from the very smallest to the most rewarding and fulfilling.

4

THE SOURCE OF MORALITY

Some imagine the morality of hedonists to be something along the lines of the idiotic slogan, "If it feels good, do it!" which basically would mean they have no morality at all, like animals. People feeling this way are often the same folks who believe morality springs solely from the rule/law/word of their God or scripture and that it's near impossible, if not entirely impossible, without it. Others think following man's laws and/or social rules are enough to be moral. But in truth, morality is something very different than just following laws, rules, scriptures, or social standards. Even some sociopaths might follow such, does that make them moral? No. At best it mimics morality but all they would really be is compliant. Compliance to the authority and standards of others, even if it's God's, is not morality. To actually be moral it must come from within, from your own inner sense of morality. For if you can't internally judge for yourself what is moral, how would you know if any particular rule, law, scripture, or standard was moral or immoral? Your God could be a demon and you wouldn't have a clue.

So, where does an "inner sense of morality" come from?

To some degree internal moral judgment can come through practical reasoning and self-interest; as to lie, cheat, steal, and harm others can be poisonous to one's own environment and have negative repercussions that bring harm to oneself. But to care about one's own self-interest requires the ability to experience pleasure and suffering in the first place. It's an absolute prerequisite, not just for that sort of morality to form but also for the more selfless and deep. It's through one's capacity to feel love, compassion and empathy that morality finds its highest expression, and those can't exist without the ability to feel pleasure and suffering in the first place. Our entire spectrum of emotions depends on it.

Since the good hedonist's path embraces love, the development of one's heart, and their connection to all - because those are sources of great pleasure - it leads naturally to the highest form of morality, not away from it.

THE FOUNDATION

The experiential states of pleasure and suffering are so fundamental we tend to take them for granted and not see how they are the primal base so many things we value are built upon. In fact, value itself depends on it! Without pleasure and suffering, value, love, compassion, virtue, morality, and justice couldn't exist. Even the basic concepts of good and bad would be impossible. All there could be is complete indifference.

While what I've just stated seems obvious to me, people have been arguing about this sort of stuff for centuries. Some say "good and bad", "right and wrong" and morality are just shifting subjective points of view floating on the self-interest and whims of human beings. What these folks miss is that all these things are much more than just "points of view". They are built upon the felt states of pleasure and suffering, which lends them a solidity and substance as firm as anything in this universe. To dismiss these felt states as anything less is to undervalue the most essential part of ourselves and trivialize our existence.

As for those that say God is the source of morality, even God would be dependent on the existence of pleasure and suffering to formulate any sort of true morality. Otherwise it would just be arbitrary rules pulled out of "his/her" cosmic ass. How moral could a completely indifferent God be? What would his/her/its morality be based on?

Hedonism and morality are not at odds; they stand on the same ground and eventually, in their fullest expression, become one.

The good hedonist knows the great value of love,
and so naturally manifests true virtue, integrity
and morality in their actions.

5

IMPULSIVE AND INDULGENT?
THE LOUSY HEDONIST

Besides amorality, the "If it feels good, do it!" slogan suggests that immediate indulgence of all urges, impulses, and desires for pleasure is the way to go. Again, like an animal.

If you raise a child by indulging it's every desire and whim, what you create is an awful, shallow, selfish brat with no skills at handling suffering, creating pleasure, or dealing with their various emotions and desires. Unhappy, vulnerable, and out of control, they are lousy hedonists with grossly unrealistic expectations. And adults practicing constant indulgence don't fare much better. It's a road leading to addictions and misery.

So, impulsive indulgence is obviously not the way to go to be a competent hedonist. What's needed is skill, discipline, and self-control. That's skill at achieving, maximizing, and maintaining pleasure, and at avoiding and overcoming suffering. Skill means having methods that work well and have no negative repercussions*. But skill without the discipline and self-control to make use of those skills is useless. Both are a must for a competent hedonist.

I know it's particularly hard to associate discipline and

---

* An extreme example of a method with negative repercussions would be using heroin. Very poor skill there!

self-control with hedonism, but to be competent at anything requires such. And, as lack of self-control can lead to much suffering and a degradation of pleasure, it's a necessity for the good hedonist.

To be a good hedonist takes skill and self-control.

6

THE BIRTHPLACE OF SUFFERING - DESIRE, WANT, NEED, AND DEMAND

Oddly, the most important skill for a good hedonist is not in generating pleasure but in dealing with suffering. I know that may seem backward, but if you are poor at dealing with suffering then your pleasure is always vulnerable to that weakness. While some may think generating pleasure can remove suffering, it often acts as only a temporary distraction or cover up, which can lead to addiction dynamics. So, to be a good hedonist requires skill at dealing directly with suffering in an effective manner, not just temporary escape from it.

Interestingly, skill at dealing with suffering is a two edged sword that's also useful at generating pleasure, since any movement away from suffering is also a movement toward pleasure. And not just toward minor pleasure, it can be applied all the way up the scale. There is no limit.

Where does one start? With their desires, wants, needs, and demands. That's the birthplace of suffering, where suffering begins. There can't be suffering without want, because suffering itself is the insistent desire to be rid of something. It's the biggest obstacle to your pleasure, enjoyment, and happiness. Which means learning to manage your desires is essential for a good hedonist. Unfortunately, it's not an easy task. Desires aren't just thoughts, they are physically felt. The thought, "I want a car" is just words in the head if there's not a corresponding feeling pulling you toward the car and away from not having the car. Desire is that pulling. If felt strong enough it might be called a need, demand, compulsion, fear, obsession, or addiction. Felt very weakly it might be called a whim or notion. Anywhere between those extremes might be called want, urge, drive, craving, wish, hope, dream, or whatever. It's all desire.

THE SUCKING SWAMP

We are a tricky mess of interconnected and intertwined desires, hopes, dreams, demands, fears, anxieties, expectations, prejudices, traumas, drives, urges, etc. It's a swamp that can suck you down a vortex that constantly declares the moment you are in is not good enough. It's the destroyer of happiness, the creator of suffering. If you are always seeing what is missing rather than appreciating what is there, you impoverish the present and alienate yourself from reality and the true fullness of the moment, effectively blocking any joy from entering.

Of course, desires aren't all bad. They serve both good and bad ends. Without desire we'd never do anything! Well, other than slowly die. Desires are essential. The basic drives to seek pleasure and escape suffering are desires; the prime desires all others are made of. Everything you desire is either to gain/maintain pleasure of some sort, or to escape/avoid suffering of some sort. Though our desires are usually experienced as a tightly combined mixture of the two, these elements are primary. And if you are up to the task of sorting them out, the "mess" can be simplified, placing all desires in one camp or the other. Trying to get pleasure or avoid suffering. One pulling toward, the other pushing away. Desire for, desire against. Want, don't want. Accepting, rejecting. Embracing, shoving away. Attraction and aversion. For simplicity right now, they could be called positive and negative desires.

Though negative desires can serve a positive purpose, like keeping you from sticking your hand in a wood chipper, by nature they generate suffering. As I previously stated, suffering itself is an insistent desire to be rid of something - a pushing away. If you felt pain yet didn't feel a desire to be rid of it, you wouldn't be suffering; you'd only be experiencing the sensation of pain. Not to get mired in semantics, but this is an important distinction. Pain itself isn't suffering, it's the wanting to be rid of that pain (or rid of whatever) that constitutes suffering. And being as we desire to be rid of the state of suffering itself, suffering can form a feedback loop that amplifies and perpetuates itself much like microphone feedback, where a sound gets amplified and re-amplified exponentially in a loop, making something small become very large and irritating.

Negative desires manifest as fear, anxiety, panic, guilt, shame, anguish, agony, anger, hate, frustration, irritation, resentment, jealousy, discomfort, despair, dread, compulsion, grasping, and every other feeling you don't like. Try to see in yourself how all of these are a physical feeling of wanting to push away, get away, or even beat away something - an aversion, rejection, or repulsion. All suffering is this same dynamic. Basically it's all a resistance to something. Resistance that doesn't just exist in the mind but is also physically felt in the body.

RESISTANCE = SUFFERING

All negative desires and suffering can be seen as *resistance*; just as all positive desires and attraction can be seen as *acceptance*. This is how I like to think of them both, as it further simplifies the whole mess and allows me to focus on how they manifest as a feeling in the body, rather than get mired in the tangled mental swamp. Acceptance as relaxing, allowing, opening, or embracing. Resistance as tension, tightening, grasping, or a pushing away. Pleasure is about acceptance. Suffering is about resistance. Simple, right?

The good hedonist sees that all suffering is resistance, and all pleasure is acceptance.

7

DISSOLVE RESISTANCE, INCREASE ACCEPTANCE

"Dissolve resistance, increase acceptance", is a simple formula to decrease suffering and increase pleasure. Right now it may sound too simplistic to be of any use, but bear with me. It is at least descriptive and focused directly on the target I want you to see.

Some resistance is deeply ingrained and stubborn. Old traumas and damage can lurk deep down in a mental black hole, sprouting fears, guilt, or anger endlessly. Dig around down there and you can easily get sucked in by its colossal gravity, or lost in a maze of mental rumination and regurgitation. The simple "dissolve resistance, increase acceptance" concept can help one avoid those quagmires. It's shorthand that can be easily remembered and used in the moment. No need to figure everything out, which is probably impossible. If you can just see or feel your suffering as resistance, then the complicated mess is translated into a very simple and tactile concept you can deal with more easily and directly. Instead of dealing with multiple complex and often hidden issues, you can deal with one simple thing you can actually physically feel, resistance. And solve it with one simple thing that can also be physically felt, acceptance. This simple tactile translation of complex internal issues has proved invaluable to me personally.

THE LESS SIMPLE - THOUGHTS

Resistance manifests in the body and the mind, as both thoughts and body sensations. They combine and intertwine to create various emotional states. While dissolving resistance can sometimes be as simple as relaxing tension in the body, other times it's necessary to look at the thought/desire/demand that's connected to that resistance and try neutralizing it one way or another. Perhaps if you gave it some thought you might realize you don't really need that desire fulfilled to be happy. You may need to confront a bullshit vision of the future you've constructed in your mind. The one where not getting that desire fulfilled is a big tragedy. If you can re-vision it as something you can accept, you're on your way. This can be difficult but usually the non-tragic version is the vastly more rational one. Though some of us have minds that prefer to crank out over-the-top drama, once that fact is recognize in yourself, it's well within your power to reign it in.

SOMETIMES IT'S NOT CRAZY TO TALK TO YOURSELF

Another method of working with thoughts is to use an affirmation type phrase, spoken internally, which promotes acceptance and letting go rather than resistance. Yes, I know affirmation sayings are usually corny, lame, or bordering on psychotic, but they really don't have to be. You can design your own to fit your particular sensibilities. I coined this one, "Don't fight the simple fact that things can't always go your way." Pretty obvious but I often need a reminder of the limits to my power and the futility of fighting pointless battles with reality. Essentially it's a more positive and de-angered version of the classic "Fuck it".

Create phrases tailored to work for you in various situations. Some asshole bending you out of shape? How about, "I can accept that assholes exist". World getting you down? How about, "I can accept that I'm not master of the universe". Hating yourself? How about, "Okay, I'm not perfect, big fucking deal". It's all about what works for you.

Another gem I've used is, "It's okay to feel like shit." You might think this would encourage suffering rather than lessen it but it doesn't. What it encourages is acceptance. By not fighting the pain it can neutralize that "feedback loop" I mentioned before. Stop that loop from forming and you can greatly lessen the intensity of your suffering, or even change its essential nature. For example, a state of agony might transform into just sadness. Which, when not resisted, can be a very tolerable, or even a beautiful expression of deep appreciation, honor, and love. Sadness doesn't have to be suffering. But when resisted, it always is.

To be a competent hedonist you need many tricks in your bag of skills. Without skill we fight unwanted events in our lives that we can't control, and as a result feel powerless. With skill we accept the unwanted events and our lack of power over them, and through that acceptance discover what powers we do have. Acceptance is the power to move from suffering to pleasure. Acceptance is the Philosopher's Stone, transforming lead into gold.

The good hedonist is able to dissolve resistance and increase acceptance.

NOW PLEASE ALLOW ME TO CLARIFY

Whatever I say will be misinterpreted or misunderstood by someone. It's unavoidable and often my own fault for being unclear. I once told a friend a little about non-resistance and he took it to mean he should indulge in all his unpleasant emotions (mainly anger) and thoughts, which he normally tried to repress. Oh course he soon got back to me with, "Hey, that non-resistance crap didn't help at all!" I had to explain he was actually indulging in resistance, not non-resistance; and that his anger and unpleasant thoughts were resistance to other issues. The mistake was mine. At the time I was just starting with this concept and had little understanding of it myself, and certainly little understanding of how others might misinterpret and misapply it. In my mind "non-resistance" was about letting go of tensions, not increasing them! But to someone used to resisting their negative feelings, "non-resistance" held another meaning altogether. That possibility hadn't entered my mind, probably because I was the opposite sort of person, accustomed to letting my anger freely flow.

Please understand that "letting go" and "letting it out" are two very different things! Anger is resistance, so if you're not resisting it you are indulging in resistance. (Not to imply that's always wrong. See below.)

There is no way to state things so perfectly clear that no one will take it the wrong way. I just try my best and hope I don't inadvertently cause any harm. Please forgive me if I do.

ANOTHER MISINTERPRETATION, OVERDOING IT

Some might go overboard with this stuff thinking they should accept everything and never resist anything. Let me clearly state here - THAT IS ASININE! And if you think non-resistance means doing whatever you have an impulse to do - YOU ARE AN IDIOT! Can you imagine if everyone practiced that what it would be like?! Half the world would die in the first month!

Context is everything. Resistance can be good or bad. Acceptance can be good or bad. Take anger. It's a form of resistance, yet can serve a good cause or a bad one. While acceptance misused might encourage passive behavior when action is called for, anger could encourage action, even bravery, in the right moment. In another situation anger could encourage awful behavior and cause great harm. Context, context, context. What is being served? Good or bad? Love or hate? Is it going toward your ultimate goal or away from it? Good judgment is essential.

The good hedonist knows when to resist and when to accept, by which best serves their ultimate goal.

8

SOMETIMES A JET
ISN'T JUST A JET

Much like the positive and negative poles of a magnet, most positive desires have a negative desire closely attached to it, and vice versa. You want health; you don't want illness. You want to eat; you don't want to be hungry. You want wisdom; you don't want ignorance. You want respect; you don't want disrespect. Want love; don't want indifference. Etc., etc., etc. They can sometimes combine so closely they seem like one thing and we hardly notice the dual nature. But it's very important to notice and clearly see the division. That way one can focus on where the trouble is created rather than make an enemy of all desire. Desire is an essential part of our being, so one should never desire to be desire-less, which would be a ridiculously contradictory state to be in! The goal of a good hedonist is not to unnaturally rid themselves of desire, but just to not let their desires cause pointless suffering or impede pleasure and happiness.

Let's take a ridiculous example. A spoiled rich guy who badly wants his own jet and is very unhappy he can't afford one like his richer friends. Obviously no one needs their own jet. He's manufactured unhappiness out of a completely unnecessary and superfluous desire. But where exactly is the suffering coming from? Where is the resistance?

He desires a jet. The attraction to a jet can't cause suffering, because attraction is a form of acceptance. So there has to be another desire, a resistance or aversion type of desire, that's attached to it generating the suffering. Perhaps being "one-upped" by his friends makes him feel insecure, which is a feeling he can't stand and resists. That could make him very uncomfortable. Insecurity is fear, and fear is unpleasant. The "negative desire" in this case would be to not feel insecure; his resistance manifesting as jealousy, discomfort and the impulsive "need" for a jet. His mind and body impulsively and subconsciously decided getting a jet is the cure for his uncomfortable feelings. If he understood it was his fear of insecurity that was causing the jealousy, want and suffering, he could work on the real issue rather than trying to solve it by buying a jet. But as is usual for such things, the real issue is seldom recognized or confronted.

Seeing the root of any particular suffering is invaluable. Getting the jet might make "jet-boy" feel better for a while but the issue would remain and undoubtedly surface again and again. The jet was a temporary solution, a distraction from the real issue. We do that all the time, with urges to eat, buy, drug, sex, control, impress, hit with a mallet, whatever.

A good hedonist doesn't chase after pleasure to escape or drown out suffering. They allow pleasure by dealing directly with suffering and getting it out of the way, weeding out their fear and resistance to life, to the present moment, and to the universe. It's that fear and resistance which holds back the vast oceans of pleasure at our disposal.

The deeper philosophical issue with jet-boy is that

essentially he is rejecting the universe he's in - the one where he can't afford a jet. That's what we all do whenever our wants and demands are strong enough to cause suffering. It says this moment, reality, world, life, universe, is not enough. By rejecting the present reality we alienate ourselves from it, thus blocking pleasure and causing suffering. Lessening the resistance in ourselves brings us closer to reality, truth, life, the present moment. And acceptance can unite us intimately with it.

That's the movement the good hedonist pursues: From resistance, fear, alienation and suffering - to acceptance, union, and bliss. To move from resistance to acceptance can take years of hard work or happen in a second with little effort. But all will run into obstacles. Most have a mass of wants, demands and fears that keep getting in the way between themselves and happiness. Even just one deeply held want can ruin your day, month, year, or life.

The good hedonist sees the dual nature of most desires and how they can obstruct happiness.

9

IF WISHES WERE DONKEYS, EVERYONE WOULD GET KICKED

The destroyer of happiness is thinking there is something you need in order to be happy. Something you don't have. That sounds simple enough, but the list of what most of us want and think we need is near endless. Let's look at one of the most loaded desires of all, the desire for a relationship. It's not one desire but a smorgasbord of inner-connected desires, drives, demands, fears, expectations, hopes and dreams. I've created a simplified sample list of typical desires one might wish or expect to get fulfilled in a relationship, coupled with their attached negative counterparts.

A RELATIONSHIP DESIRE GROUP

WANTS/ATTRACTIONS	DON'T WANT/AVERSIONS
A good relationship	None or bad relationship
Love	Indifference
Companionship	Loneliness, isolation
Loyalty	Betrayal, abandonment

Acceptance, validation	Rejection, feeling unwanted
Happiness	Unhappiness
Security	Insecurity
Respect	Disrespect
Sex	No sex
Intimacy	Distance, isolation
To be treated well	To be abused
Power, control	Powerlessness
Dreams fulfilled	Dreams crushed
Expectations met	Disappointment

Some things in the DON'T WANT column might be inflamed by damage left behind from various traumas one has suffered over the years. Even if long forgotten, they still can be a big influence. The greater the damage, the more "loaded" and intense these aversions will be.

The things in the WANT column are often charged with the feeling that having them will heal past trauma or solve some current suffering. If you feel you really NEED something, it's usually about past damage or current suffering and the fear you have of things in the DON'T WANT column. An aversion can latch on to an attraction, infecting and transforming it into a NEED or DEMAND. Attraction is normally a pleasant state, but infected by aversion it becomes infused with suffering.

Attraction and aversion can intertwine and mix so thoroughly they feel like one thing. This is how a naturally joyous attraction becomes an unpleasant aching or longing we can hardly stand; which is why we have the term "love sick".

Our aversions are where suffering is manufactured. So obviously, learning to better handle our aversions and keep them from poisoning our attractions is a prime skill for a good hedonist.

Make your own list of desires, both "wants" and "don't wants", and try to imagine what it would be like if you didn't fear any of the things in the "Don't Want" column (not to imply they aren't valid fears). How would that change your experience? How does a desire feel when it's purely attraction with no aversions attached to or mixed in with it?

The good hedonist sees how aversions create suffering and can infect our attractions.

OTHER FORCES MUCKING ABOUT

There's more to the picture I shouldn't leave out.

1. MOTHER NATURE IS A BITCH

Of course Nature manipulates our desires mercilessly. The tricks it pulls to get us to mate-up, breed, and raise our young are devious and powerful. Hormones, endorphins, and other bio-blackjacks chemically beating us into line for Mother Nature's propagation blitzkrieg. It's no wonder we can go so nuts in relationships! It's a lot to deal with.

2. MISSING THE PACK

I'm sure the fact our species survived for many millennia bonding in small hunter-gatherer groups has a big effect on us too. We modern humans have lost too much of that sense of belonging, purpose and validation the small tribal group once provided. So we often look to the bond of a romantic relationship to fulfill all that the tribal bond once provided; which is asking a bit much of it.

3. CULTURE

Of course there's also the fact our culture keeps beating into us the message/image of the ideal romantic relationship. As a result we can feel like sad losers missing out on the greatest thing in life if we don't have a relationship anywhere near that ballpark; and especially if we have no relationship at all.

We've been trained (at least here in the USA) to have very high expectations, not just in relationships but in nearly all aspects of life. It's nearly impossible to fulfill even one of them, let alone all. This sets us up for much frustration, disappointment, and despair.

AND HERE WE SIT

All together it's a lot of pressure. It's no wonder relationships fail so often and depression rates are so high! So please, cut yourself and everyone else some slack. Lots of it.

Regardless of the origins and history, the entire mess

is expressed as our desires. They are the tactile connection we feel to all that squirms beneath the surface. And it's where we can effect great change in our daily experience of suffering and pleasure.

The good hedonist understands the forces at work within and how to navigate and manage them.

10

DEMANDS AND ACCEPTING THE UNACCEPTABLE

Anything you "must have" or "must not have" is a demand. Essentially it's a model you hold of what is required to be happy. When reality doesn't match the demanded model, a separation and alienation between you and reality is created. This can manifest as many different unpleasant emotions. These are the loaded issues that have us rejecting our life, hating the world, and fearing the future. Demands are a futile rebellion against what is, creating a prison which blocks out light and joy. All they accomplish is to fan fears, amplify suffering, block pleasure, and mislead one from real solutions.

Demands are about resistance, a desire to avoid suffering of some sort. Whether the result of trauma, or a screwed up model of reality, demands are a solid block of resistance to something. They can lurk hidden below the surface or plainly in view, making the present intolerable and the future appear a nightmare.

A demand says that something is completely unacceptable to you. This makes demands very hard to dislodge and overcome. How exactly does one accept what they believe is totally unacceptable?

It may seem impossible but it's not. Nearly all demands are flawed in some substantial way. They present themselves as certainties or facts when in truth they are usually exaggerations, half-truths, all-out lies, or based on false premises. Demands present things as an "either or" situation but it never really is. Much like the delusions of a paranoid, demands create unnecessary drama and fear, forcing one into a dance of suffering.

At the heart of any demand is an unwillingness - be it manifest as fear or any other sort of resistance - to face a particular form of suffering, which is represented and stored in our mind as a thought/image, an idea. It's in that idea that the flaw will reside. Identify what that is and you'll have a good chance to resolve the issue and get rid of the demand and its poisonous effects.

Perhaps you think you don't make demands. It may not be obvious, because demands are often unspoken, hidden under the surface in our subconscious and only recognized by the negative emotional reactions they produce in us. Anytime you get upset with someone or something it's because of a demand you harbor. If there wasn't a demand you wouldn't get upset. The emotion is expressing that something is unacceptable to you. An expectation or desire is not met and rather than accepting it we fight it. That resistance is our "demand", manifested as emotion. And what we are fighting is reality.

The good hedonist makes few demands and is always willing to face truth.

DON'T GO NUTS! THERE ARE GOOD DEMANDS!

Here's where I need to point out that some "demands" are good. One might get a bit carried away and think they should never have ANY demands. In other words, be in a state of constant ACCEPTANCE while harboring no demands whatsoever. But that's really not such a stellar idea. Some demands and resistance serve good positive purposes; such as resistance to injustice, or a demand against rape. Keep that in mind! What to aim for is just to avoid all the negative demands that accomplish nothing positive and only serve suffering. Good demands, that serve the greater goals and values of the good hedonist, are to be embraced.

The good hedonist knows which demands to ignore and which to embrace.

CONTROL ISSUES

Demands are about control. We are trying to force our will onto reality. So all we need to do to overcome our demands is to do the opposite and accept reality as it is. That means we face what we were unwilling to face and accept what we were unwilling to accept. This is our greatest power to change our reality. Because though we don't have the power to grant all our demands, we do have the power to not make those demands.

I think most of us would like it if we would generally get less upset rather than more, right? So it's usually a good thing, within certain parameters of course, to be less "demanding" of conditions, situations, or the behavior of others.

Great strides can be made by simply accepting the limits of our control. Be it over the behavior and actions of others or ourselves, events in the universe, or the past, present or future. By accepting our limits we can discover our true power. Suffering is created within, not without, and our demands are a part of that process. It all comes back to suffering being resistance and acceptance being the cure.

The good hedonist accepts the limits of his/her power and control.

EXAMPLE A

A failed marriage or relationship is a very difficult thing to accept and causes great suffering. This is a good example of a "demand". A demand is not measured by the amount of desire for a relationship to succeed, but by the amount of resistance to it failing. Some go so far as murder and/or suicide to stop a reality they can't accept. Their demand is so strong they reject life itself when the demand is not met. But even with much weaker demands there is an element of us rejecting life or reality because it's not measuring up. This all produces suffering. Suffering that could be avoided with adequate skill at dissolving demands and accepting facts/reality.

When we resist suffering we only make it stronger. It's like one of those Chinese finger traps, the harder you try to pull your fingers out, the harder it holds on. So our natural inclination to pull away proves, in this situation, to be counterproductive and work against us. The way to overcome suffering is not by trying to fight it, push it away or run from it, but rather by turning toward it without fear and accepting that it is there. Acceptance allows its hold to ease and release. Demands make it tighten.

One way to find some acceptance to the "unacceptable" is to put it in a greater context. Can you accept that failed marriages/relationships exist? Can you accept being in a world that allows failed marriages/relationships to exist? Then why are you so special they should never happen to you? Isn't it ridiculous to demand to be exempt from such?

Reality can either be accepted or rejected. When we are unable or unwilling to accept our reality we retreat into denial, frustration, anger, resentment, jealousy, depression, despair, fear, guilt, anxiety, etc. It's obviously a poor strategy. Our resistance ends up creating more suffering than facing reality would. That's why the good hedonist must find the courage to embrace the reality they are in. Not that one must become a tough-guy or stoic martyr, but rather, wise enough to recognize what's in their own best interest. Accepting the reality you are in is fundamental to approaching happiness.

Accept truth. Don't make demands against it. And don't demand to never feel vulnerable, disappointed, lonely, sad or grieving. They are not enemies to be feared or fought. It's only our resistance which turns them into enemies.

The good hedonist embraces reality, accepting difficult truths along with the easy ones, expecting no special treatment.

THE SHORT ANSWER FOR WHEN LIFE DOESN'T COOPERATE AND YOU REALLY MUST FIND A WAY TO ACCEPT WHAT YOU THOUGHT WAS UNACCEPTABLE

When life denies you the things you want most it can be very hard to accept. One way to find that acceptance is to realize that the thing or things you are "demanding" in order to be happy are only a means to an end, not the end itself. The actual goal is to achieve a satisfying level of sustained enjoyment and happiness: a fulfilled state. If you've convinced yourself that you must have certain things to reach that level of happiness, then you have set up a structure which acts as an obstacle to happiness. And because it acts as a resistance to any reality where those desires are not met, it generates suffering in response to any of those realities. The thought itself is a suffering generator. So change the thought.

What needs to be understood is that you can have the level of enjoyment and happiness you seek without the thing desired/demanded. It's an illusion that you must have that thing to be happy. And that illusion can keep you from happiness. Once you understand those facts you will be better able to let go of the demand and embrace the reality wherein that demand is not met. In other words, you will be able to "accept the unacceptable". That frees you from the resistance and suffering that the unmet demands were generating; which in turn naturally increases your level of enjoyment and happiness, putting you closer to your real goal.

The good hedonist knows the true goal and so doesn't get sidetracked and trapped by false ones.

11

FEAR

Though we'd all like to be fearless, that actually would be a very bad idea. Fear is needed; otherwise our species would never have survived. It's a very important part of our survival/self-protection instinct. Unfortunately, it also can cause us much unnecessary suffering, effectively blocking our ability to experience happiness, express love, or embrace life. So the good hedonist must learn to detect and overcome fears that serve them poorly.

Fear, resistance and demands are all aspects of one thing. Demands form around fears, and fear is a form of resistance. Lessening any one of the three will lessen the others, and lessen suffering.

Fear can manifest in many different forms, from full-blown panic to just being slightly uncomfortable. Lots of the stress and tension we harbor are about fear. So weeding out fears and gaining more control over the fear instinct is part of the process of decreasing resistance/suffering and increasing acceptance/pleasure. Of course one shouldn't strive to become free of all fear, as I said, it's needed. The goal is just to keep it firmly within a rational context and not let it congeal into unnecessary suffering.

Many of our fears don't actually cause us much suffering, because they don't come up very often. If you fear flying you can simply avoid flying, or just suffer for the limited time you're actually on a plane. It's not something you must get rid of to have a very enjoyable life. The biggest concern for the good hedonist is the systemic fears that constantly undermine one's enjoyment. Often these are fears you aren't even aware you have, lurking in the background, causing resistance that can manifest in a million different ways.

For example, if you have a deep set fear of abandonment it might manifest as distrust, jealousy, anger, insecurity, shyness, worry, anxiousness, paranoia, panic, unhappiness, depression, tension, stress, negativity, demands, being controlling, submissiveness, clinginess, pushing people away, falling "in love" too easily, fear of love, fear of intimacy, fear of commitment, hating everyone, hating yourself, hating the world, hating cute little puppies, etc.

One deeply set fear can poison your entire life. It's like that saying, "When you're wearing shoes, the entire world is covered in shoe leather". A single fear might affect how you see and react to almost everything; coloring not just your behavior but your vision of yourself, others and the world. So removing that fear would have profound and far reaching effects.

Of course, removing fear is easier said than done. You can't just force it away; you have to find a way to bring acceptance to it. And to do that it helps to know what you're afraid of, which isn't always apparent. The object of one's fear may be stealthily hidden and signs of its presence only subtle discomforts, like a hollow feeling or a nagging unease or impatience. Stronger emotional responses make it more obvious, but even while in a full-blown panic attack you may still be unaware of what exactly it is you're afraid of.

From my own experience I know how clueless one can be. It took me months to figure out what my own panic attacks were about. Hell, it took a month before I even realized they were panic attacks! Dumb as I may be, part of the problem is our fear and panic responses come from the older "reptilian" part of our brains, so our higher brain functions can be completely out of the loop and mystified by what's going on. Finding yourself in a strong fear/panic response and not knowing what the object of the fear is can be extremely confusing and scare you even more. But it does teach you how devious and hidden your fears can be.

The "reptilian" brain has two well-known basic reactions to any perceived threat. You've heard it many times, "fight or flight". Which I guess made perfect sense millions of years ago, but nowadays, not so much. Those two standard visceral reactions are the engine driving a plethora of emotional and psychological states. They are the essence of resistance and can chronically lurk below the surface, acting like an acid eating away at your contentment.

Systemic fears can be so subtle and constant they're invisible, camouflaged in normality. Like background radiation, it's background fear that's constantly undermining your enjoyment. Unfortunately there's no equivalent of a radiation detector for fear. All we have is our own powers of self-examination to figure things out.

One can be aware they have a certain fear but unaware of the ways it's affecting them. An extremely jealous person may not connect their jealousy with their fear of abandonment. And that's an obvious one! Even when something is right in front of your face, you still need to open your mind to see it.

Behind any systemic fear there's usually some damage from a past trauma. But don't get bogged down focusing on history and stirring old shit up. It's absolutely futile to fight the past. Let the past be, or even better, let it go. Accept it as shit that happened. Just concern yourself with the current fear, resistance and demands that have resulted from that damage.

Resistance hangs on to suffering, acceptance allows it to pass. It's not necessary to identify where that suffering originally came from to let it go. Just understand it's a relic, a ghost haunting the present that there is no need to hang on to, and good reason to let go of.

Try to lessen the demands that have formed around the fear/resistance. Often they are blatantly unreasonable, like a demand to never experience any disappointment. Approach it more from the stance of accepting reality rather than removing fear or damage. You are lessening your resistance to reality, which is vain resistance. And that brings less fear, less demands, and less suffering.

Another fear generating problem is the mind's projection of imagined negative results. It can amplify danger and stoke fear by creating unrealistically bleak or tragic images of what will be if certain demands are not met, compulsively filling you with overly dramatic scenarios of an unacceptable future. It's important to become aware of your mind's creative nonsense and recognize it as the overblown bullshit it is. Like a bad movie scrip, you shouldn't take it too seriously. It can help to simply imagine a scenario where your demand is not met and everything is okay. Or one where you have the courage to face your future, whatever it is.

The process of lessening fear takes work. Fears need to be recognized. Denials overcome. Old suffering let go of. Demands reassessed. Realities accepted. Courage cultivated. The scary projections your mind creates confronted and reeled in.

And here's the kicker to all this: If you fear suffering, then you will have millions of things to fear. So just by lessening your fear of suffering itself you can lessen a million obstacles to your happiness. It's quite a bargain.

To fear pain and suffering is to be controlled by them. So the good hedonist strives to have courage.

12

WHY I DIDN'T OFF MYSELF
PANIC FOR DUMMIES

For two years I had a constant urge to off myself. Fortunately, I had absolutely no intention of following through on such an extreme course of action. It seemed a dumb idea (most of the time), yet it was still there pestering me. So what the hell was going on?

When I closely examined the feeling I could see it was a constant low grade feeling of panic, and the object of the panic/fear was the world, or rather a vision of the world, which appeared to be unacceptably awful. This wasn't my intellectual model but a vision that lurked more below the surface than above. Pulling this stuff into the light helped me find ways to deal with the situation. I could see the suicidal urge was really just an urge to escape the paranoid bullshit vision of the world my mind was excreting underneath the surface, like a boil. So, discrediting and undermining the veracity of that vision was a way to lessen and dissolve the fear/panic I was feeling. This experience helped clarify how easily my mind could undermine my happiness and produce suffering. Luckily the reverse is just as true.

The good hedonist becomes familiar with the various ways their mind can produce suffering, and so gains skill against them.

CORNERED

Panic is felt when what you fear is upon you. It's a cornered feeling, a dire urge for escape that can drive you up a wall. If you feel cornered by life itself and it appears your enemy, then a suicidal urge might present itself. It's the mind's desperate grasping for an escape route; the "reptilian" flight solution. A visceral or emotional urge that one's higher brain function may feel overwhelmed by. That older "reptilian" part of our brain can be very powerful.

Below are four things to consider in such a situation.

1. It's just "the mind's desperate grasping for an escape route". Why should you give any weight to what a panicked, desperate, grasping and probably irrational and delusional mind churns out? I always reserve the right to ignore the crap my brain regurgitates. Be it from the old "reptilian" brain or more sophisticated parts. Both are capable of grandly stupid or ridiculous things. So recognize the suicidal urge for what it usually is; stupid nonsense generated from the irrational depths of a panicked and delusional mind. It's sort of like one those movies where a mega-computer is put in control of everything and it decides the human race needs to be wiped out. Know when your computer is on the fritz.

2. The dark and hopeless image of reality that you are seeing is not actual reality; it's just a creation of your mind while in an off-kilter state (see "The Shit Hole"). Well, assuming you aren't actually physically trapped

in some actual inescapable Hell-on-Earth. The vast majority of suicidal people are not. Usually it's their mind creating a false hell-scape out of fairly normal problems. So, face or dismiss the boogieman your mind has created. It's just a thought, an image, not actual reality. Rest assured that true reality is much better than the freak show your mind is presenting that has you so desperate. You don't need to physically escape reality; you just need to change your mind's image of reality, which seems a much less drastic course than offing yourself!

3. You can't really know what suicide might lead to. Are you that sure there's no afterlife, or if there is it will better? What if your state of mind just follows you there, so you'd be just as miserable in some other realm? What if it's a worse torture than what you're trying to escape? If you felt trapped before just think how much worse it could get, stuck in a netherworld with no physical body and perhaps nothing to do but stew about what a mistake killing yourself was! An eternity of regret? There's plenty of awful possibilities. Not that I take them all very seriously, or seriously at all, but it's still a huge gamble with no fallback position. Seems much better to play out the hand you've got than to gamble so recklessly. Well, like I said before, unless you're in some truly physically dire situation and not just the usual sort of bullshit people kill themselves over. The usual being stuff that could be cured by acceptance, a mere attitude change.

4. There's a lot to be said for *perseverance*. You don't know what exactly your future will hold. And as a

general rule, most suffering will eventually subside. So, simply waiting it out is an option. Of course it's better if you're actively working on it, since it may improve much faster and leave you with tools for dealing with any future episodes. But sometimes the very best we can manage is to just persevere.

My condition got better very slowly. Occasionally a bit of it will pop back up but I no longer feel helpless like I did when it first made its unwelcome appearance. Now I understand it better and have various ways to deal with it and put it in its place. Most are represented above or elsewhere in this book, but there is one specific tool I used when things were quite bad that I haven't mentioned - video games. Let's call them a "perseverance aid". I found them to be involving enough to drown out my panic and anxiety and give me some much needed temporary relief. Pure distraction. I know that elsewhere I poopoo using distraction to drown out suffering, preferring that it be dealt with directly, but sometimes you need a break; especially when you're in a long term constant negative state. You can't be working on it all the goddamned time. Perhaps you could find an activity to fill the bill that was more wholesome and beneficial than video games: Recreational interests, sports, hobbies, music, movies, books, food, friends, robots, new lint weaving business, reanimating the dead, whatever. I had a few other things that worked to a degree, but they all had practical limitations and weren't as reliable or as efficient as video games. Video games were always at hand, under my control, and worked every time. Well, long as the power was on.

Of course there's some risk of getting addicted, and I probably was, but next to my other problem that seemed a very minor issue that was vastly outweighed by the benefit I was getting. And it's ridiculously less risky than prescribed medications.

One thing I'd advise against using in this manner is recreational drugs or alcohol, because the danger of them making matters worse is simply too great. Not to say all drugs hold the same amount of danger, but when you're so close to the edge already it's not the time to risk indulging in anything with the potential to push you even a tiny bit further in a negative direction. Usually that comes with any drug comedown, hangover or addiction, but even the high can be very dangerous, because the last thing any suicidal person needs is something that lowers their inhibitions or helps create delusional states.

Keep in mind all the above is addressing only my own limited experiences. I humbly admit my ignorance beyond that scope and offer my sympathy and apologies to those that have more serious suicidal urges or ones with different underpinnings than what I described here.

The good hedonist perseveres.

13

DEPRESSION

Obviously, depression is something for a good hedonist to avoid! Hopefully this book provides some tools that are useful toward that end. After all, depression is mostly just a big sticky wad of resistance that has reached critical mass. So every tool for working with resistance can be applied to depression. But there are a few other things to say about the issue.

First is about the way "depression" is now commonly portrayed as merely a problem of brain chemistry. This benefits the pharmaceutical industry more than the folks with depression. While depression can be a matter of our chemistry being thrown out of whack by various things, much more commonly it's about psychological or emotional factors and our own weaknesses in coping with various events and realities in our lives. People can get stuck in negative ways of thinking and overwhelmed by failures, disappointments, tragedies, stresses, etc. Merely throwing drugs at these issues is not the best strategy. Certainly there are times and circumstances where medication is called for and helpful, but in this current tsunami of medicating it's very clear that things have gotten way out of hand. And since none of the drugs used is without substantial complications and dangers, and work little better than placebos, it's a very ugly situation. We want to trust science but in this case science plays a secondary role to the marketplace and greed. Profit is why these drugs are created and the FDA does a poor job of enforcing high scientific standards.

"Depression" is not a singular "disease" but rather just a general term that denotes a collection of various symptoms and says absolutely nothing about the cause or causes. Nothing. This is an important distinction to make. By giving a simple "disease" label to a complex reality, it can keep one from seeing what is truly going on. If you think your problem is a disease called "depression" then you won't be looking at the real issues that are the actual cause of your problem, and will be more likely to seek only medical solutions (mainly drugs). This puts the focus on symptoms and chemistry, not root causes or lasting solutions.

Depression is not just about being a mess internally. Some of it is normal reactions to fucked-up situations. I think it's clear our society itself is causing much of this pandemic of "depression". With "the rat race" and "dog eat dog" being such common expressions for the society we've built, it's no wonder we aren't all so happy. No amount of medicating can fix that.

Don't fret. The good hedonist is better equipped to overcome these obstacles, and to learn from them. As you build your skills, tools, and experience, a state of "depression" will become less likely and less threatening. Acceptance is our sword and armor.

Of course a depressed person might think they are "accepting" the true hopelessness of their life and are the one actually facing facts and reality. They'd be confusing *believing* with *accepting*. Basically they are believing in their resistance and its accompanying vision of "reality". To actually accept a "hopeless" life would be to *embrace* it, which is definitely not what any depressed person is doing.

The good hedonist is always learning, and applies all he/she has learned to overcome all obstacles.

14

HAPPINESS

The way to be happy is not by trying to get all you desire, but by appreciating all you have in this moment. That doesn't mean to mull over the list of all you currently possess but rather to focus fully on the moment at hand and embrace it as it is, appreciating it's unique character and gifts.

I think most can agree with the above statement, though following it is another story. We are just so used to the habit of reaching for happiness through our desires it's hard to do anything else, even when seeing the wisdom of it. Such ingrained behavior can't be changed overnight but only through prolonged effort and the slow work of developing new habits. For that to happen certain facts must be thoroughly driven into one's skull.

1. Our capacity to want is endless, so fulfilling desires can be an endless treadmill going nowhere. Soon as you fulfill one, another springs up to take its place, keeping one in a constant state of striving and want.

2. Focusing on desires keeps one's sight on what's missing rather than that what is there, thus imprisoning one in a constant state of lacking.

3. Many desires are beyond our power to fulfill, such

as the desire to be loved or the desire to not be hurt. And in this modern world there are a colossal amount things to want beyond our reach, so it's very easy to end up with quite a backlog of unfulfilled desires clogging us up with disappointment, frustration and despair; keeping happiness at bay.

4. Chasing desires limits your happiness to only those moments your desires are met enough to cause you to stop striving and start embracing the moment. Which is no sure thing and may be very short lived. So why not eliminate the middleman and go right to embracing the moment?

I'll repeat that - Why not eliminate the middleman and go right to embracing the moment? That is the most direct way to happiness, though not always within our reach. However, it is a skill one can learn. Each little bit of resistance you dissolve, and each little bit of acceptance you muster, will lead you there. Happiness itself is a certain level of acceptance and appreciation, so the path to it is by moving away from resistance and discontent, which is a substantial part of most desires.

If "embracing the moment" sounds a bit too precious or is asking too much, then "accepting the moment" or "allowing the moment" will do. Whatever you can muster in that direction is a win.

Having this more direct way to achieve happiness - independent from and superior to the unreliable, messy and often counterproductive method of satisfying desires - is essential for the good hedonist.

The good hedonist realizes the biggest obstacle to one's happiness is thinking you need something to be happy.

ALWAYS WITHIN REACH

Both happiness and misery are created from within, not from without. Which doesn't mean you are to blame or the world isn't, just that it's an internal process and there's nothing outside yourself you need to add to create happiness. Pleasure, happiness, bliss are all always available within, if you can find or create it. Even if you are living alone in a cardboard box and have only a week left to live, it's still the way you are thinking and reacting to it inside yourself, your fear and resistance, that causes misery, not the situation itself directly. That's not to say there aren't times misery is called for and a perfectly legitimate or proper way to feel. The point is just that suffering and pleasure are generated internally, not externally, so we always have access to the mechanics of both misery and happiness within our reach. It's only our lack of skill which limits us.

If we are always looking to something outside ourselves to be happy we are vulnerable to the extreme fickleness of good fortune, the unpredictability of our own reactions, and the substantial limitations of our power to manipulate the outside world. Happiness always starts right here, inside yourself, with what you have now in this moment. So that is where one should go to find it.

The good hedonist knows that pleasure and suffering are created within, not from without; and so that is where their greatest power lies.

THE SHORT VERSION

Happiness is when we are in the state of embracing the moment.

Unhappiness is when we are resisting/rejecting the moment.

The good hedonist knows the way to happiness is not through desires but through the acceptance and embrace of this moment.

15

FORGIVENESS AND BLAME

Forgiveness is a way to let go of negative emotions such as anger, hate and resentment. In other words, it helps dissolve resistance and increase acceptance. So it's of great value to the good hedonist.

1. FORGIVING OTHERS

When it comes to forgiving others, try to understand that no one chose to be what they are. Neither the wonderful person or the total asshole, the saint or the megalomaniac, chose to be such. Though one can choose to do good or bad in any particular situation, everything within themselves which goes into making that choice is not a choice at all. Does anyone choose to have a conscience or compassion and empathy? How about to be greedy, shallow, or heartless? No, the degree to which we possess any of those things is quite beyond our control. The amounts of good and bad attributes in us are not by our own design. None of us gets to pick exactly who they will be or what flaws or qualities they will have. Whatever choices you make in life, it's because you had that propensity in the first place, not because you simply *willed* it.

Our supposed "free will" really isn't all that free. All it basically does is choose pleasure over suffering. It may seem more complex but if you look below the mind's profuse machinations all you'll find is that primal drive behind every choice. It's easy to mistake the thinking mind for the will because one's will is so intimately connected to and tangled up in the mind's vast fountain of thought. Our minds can imagine, remember, judge, project into the future, use language, and operate below our conscious level. It's quite an overwhelming show, so it's no wonder our will gets lost in it.

The will is felt, not thought. It's most directly seen through your feelings of acceptance or resistance, and all the combinations thereof. The thinking mind is more a tool, servant or deranged troublemaker than the seat of your will. I know what I'm saying may be hard to swallow for some, but perhaps you've had the experience of your thoughts keeping you from sleeping and not being able to shut them down no matter how hard you tried. In moments like that, when thoughts out-right defy your will, it's pretty clear they have a certain independence. While your thinking mind can express your will, it also can manipulate, frustrate, mislead, or defy it.

The quality of the choices we make and our behavior depends heavily on the quality of our minds, which is something beyond our control. Another factor is the degree of empathy and compassion we possess, which is also beyond our control. And certainly none of us chose to have the basic drive toward pleasure and away from suffering in the first place, which is central to our will. So where is the "free" in freewill, and how responsible are we for our condition and actions?

Minds can inadvertently go haywire and generate malignant thoughts that manipulate us in bad ways. Paranoid thoughts can present false dangers that we may react to as if real. Can this be called a "freewill" if it's so easily misled and a pawn to unwanted thoughts? Perhaps, but no one wants or would choose to be a victim of a crazy brain, yet many are. Where then is their "freewill?" Do we create our own minds? Can I blame and condemn anyone for the misfortune of having a defective mind? Can I blame anyone for whatever mind they have, good or bad?

While all should be held accountable for their actions, on the grand scale of things, all are innocents. Just as no one would blame a short person for being short, or a "developmentally challenged" person for being what they are, in truth we are ALL in that same boat. We all have our own shortcomings and developmental challenges which we didn't ask for, create or deserve. Not a one of us is perfect. Are we to blame for that?

As I see it, everyone has a case for being granted some level of forgiveness and grace. Everyone.

That doesn't mean you should absolve anyone of their crimes or offenses. Bad behavior deserves and should receive appropriate responses. Always reserve the right to freely judge and discern the quality and character of each individual and their actions, and treat them accordingly. Forgiveness need only exist somewhere within your heart, not necessarily in your outward actions. One can simultaneously forgive someone in the grand scale of the universe and eternity, but not in the smaller scale of earthbound immediacy. What should definitely be avoided is holding grand scale condemnation and hate in your heart.

Forgiveness doesn't mean you have to like that person, it can come through recognition of the limitations of our power, the precariousness of our situation, and that our flaws are never eternal, all falling away to dust at some point. The whims of circumstance could favor or curse any one of us. We are all in this strange predicament together.

I find when I deeply hate and condemn someone it ends up harming me, like a nagging rash or inflamed boil. But when I extend to them an amount of forgiveness, even a tiny bit, it relieves me of that burden and I feel better. Purely on a selfish level, forgiveness is a good, practical, and welcome thing. It decreases your suffering, thus increasing your pleasure; because hate, anger, and condemnation are resistance and cause separation, while forgiveness brings a degree of acceptance and union.

THE EXTEMELY HORRIBLE

As for the most extremely horrible among us, mass murderers and such, they are examples of just how broken and twisted a human being can be. It's a depressing reality that it's even possible for such abominations to exist. It exposes and warns how fragile a construction we are, and how important compassion and empathy is to humanity and our happiness. The only forgiveness I can manage to scrape up for such creatures is in the fact they didn't create themselves or ask to be such.

The good hedonist forgives by understanding the limits of our so-called "free will" and the precariousness of the predicament we are all in.

2. FORGIVING YOURSELF AND THE HORSE YOU RODE IN ON

Personally, I really don't experience much guilt, shame or self-loathing. I get by on disappointment, regret, embarrassment, and cursing at myself. But I always forgive myself because I know in truth I didn't create my flaws. Blame the Universe, God, nature, evolution, the Big Bang, bad luck, circumstances, fate, butterflies, or whatever. Things unfold as they unfold. To embrace reality you must embrace that you're not perfect. That means you must forgive yourself and the horse you rode in on.

Forgiving yourself can be a bit trickier than forgiving others, because this jackass follows you around wherever you go! It's a problem of proximity. You can forgive others at a comfortable distance, but you're stuck with yourself constantly. So to effectively forgive yourself it requires the ability to like, or at least tolerate yourself to an acceptable degree. Otherwise you'll still be at war with yourself and miserable.

I've found that serious self-haters often hold themselves to unreasonable standards, not allowing themselves normal human feelings, thoughts, motivations, reactions, or flaws. Somehow a twisted or unreasonable model of how they should and shouldn't be has been driven into their skull. Not being able to live up to that standard fills them with guilt, shame, and self-hate, which in turn causes them to behave badly and create even more guilt, shame, and self-hate. A vicious circle.

An example would be someone who thinks they should never be selfish. Since we, as separate human beings, are all to a degree naturally and primarily selfish, such a standard is impossible and can do nothing but cause intense inner conflict and perhaps drive a person nuts. For a person like that to forgive or like themselves they must first understand the fallacy of their beliefs and then be able to embrace the truth of who they truly are. Which might be very difficult, because the truth turns out to be something they've always believed is very wrong and shameful. Forgiveness entails reordering and remaking their map/model of reality. Not an easy process, but doable.

There was a study of homophobes that found the worst offenders were often actually gay themselves but in complete denial of the fact and deeply ashamed of their same-sex attractions. Their self-repression, intolerance and hate was acted out on others. This shows how connected our self-condemnation and our condemning of others can be. It's a two way street. Finding out how to accept and forgive yourself or others is really the same thing. What applies to them, applies to you.

SOMETIMES IT'S GOOD TO HATE YOURSELF

Of course there are all sorts. Some may beat themselves up to clear their conscience in a somewhat ritualistic self-flagellation they falsely imagine pays for their crimes. And some may pretend to hate themselves in a show designed to get sympathy and appear less horrible. It's a mixed bag and I really don't want to help them all. Some are just truly awful people who should hate themselves.

You've probably met people who are much too good at forgiving themselves. They repeatedly do awful things and still think they are wonderful. These folks could definitely benefit from more self-hate, guilt, and shame. It might help them learn to stop doing awful things and become better people, which would both improve their lives and the lives of all around them.

For any of us there are times that certain amounts of self-hate, guilt, or shame can play an important positive role in getting us to recognize and try to avoid certain behaviors or actions that serve us poorly. It's a motivator and if it's working right it should help you clean up your act, thus earning your own forgiveness. Simple.

THE USELESS UNDERCURRENT

With the benefits of some self-condemnation acknowledged, and the undeserving set aside, there's still a mountain of self-condemnation that serves no good purpose and we'd all be better off without.

Most people are not exceptionally awful and don't have a major problem with self-condemnation or hate because they don't really do anything very bad. But there's hardly a one of us that doesn't wish they were better in some way. All nominally lucid and rational people know they have shortcomings and could be improved, as none of us are perfect. So though you may be fairly happy with who you are, usually there still are pockets of disappointment, regret and discontent regarding yourself. These form an undercurrent of resistance and rejection which keeps one from fully accepting and embracing themselves. This impedes the path to deeper experiences of happiness and joy. So whether you have a major self-hate issue or just a very subtle self-discontent, both are an obstacle on the good hedonist's path that can be overcome through forgiveness.

Self-forgiveness isn't about being pleased with or full of yourself. It's to dissolve inner resistance and approach deeper levels of acceptance and union. Just as to fully embrace the present moment we must first forgive it of its shortcomings, so too it is with ourselves and everything. In the grand scheme of things there is absolutely no one to blame and it comes down to forgiving reality or not forgiving reality. Can you forgive reality and embrace it as it is?

The good hedonist understands the great value of forgiveness in creating acceptance.

3. FORGIVING HUMANITY

I've noticed there are quite a few people that look down on humanity with disdain and the ugly stink of superiority; which makes little sense to me, since they themselves are a part of humanity. I suppose they think a few superior beings like themselves manage to fight their way out of nature's blighted womb against the odds. If you think you're one of those lucky souls I've got a message for you: You really aren't all that special and the term "arrogant jackass" probably fits you quite well. Welcome to the lowly masses of us imperfect human beings!

How can I be so certain they aren't as special as they think? Because their attitude reveals flaws they obviously have, so though they may be special in certain ways they are quite lacking in other ways. Arrogance, lack of humility, lack of compassion, poor insight, and poor judgment are right out in the open for all to see. Well, all to see but themselves of course.

Look, if you are actually superior in some ways to an average person then understand this: You are simply lucky and did absolutely nothing to deserve your good fortune. So don't get all puffed up about it! And have some fucking compassion for the less fortunate! If you lack that compassion then you really aren't so special after all. I don't care how brilliant you may be, without compassion you're a douche. Any truly superior person would not be arrogantly looking down on the rest of humanity. Period.

We all need to embrace the fact that we are right down in the mud with everyone else. We forgive humanity by not holding it apart from ourselves.

The good hedonist does not hold themselves apart from humanity.

4. FORGIVING THE UNIVERSE

To embrace reality fully one must find a way to forgive the Universe for its horrors. There's just no denying it can be an extremely horrid place. Like a deranged torture circus; cold, harsh, and grotesque.

Many believe in religious models that explain away the ugliness in various ways. Karma, reincarnation, sin, evil, Satan, demons, disobedience, God's tough love or punishment or anger, not sacrificing enough virgins, evil criminal alien ghosts lodged in our being, whatever. None of them work for me because none hold up well to any scrutiny.

What I see plainly is this: For anything to exist, its opposite must also exist. One defines and implies the other. Light and dark. Up and down. Expansion and contraction. Cold and hot. Beauty and ugliness. Love and hate. Pleasure and suffering. You can't have one without the other. In that case the horror in the Universe wouldn't be its measure but rather a necessary counterpoint to its opposite. Eliminate one and the other goes too. So, to rid the Universe of all bad would mean all good must go too. There's just no way around it. Allow one, you allow the other.

Of course it's much more complicated than just that, because none of these paired opposites can exist in a complete void. They all depend on a slew of other things. Probably everything depends on everything else: the entire ball of wax being one huge interdependent construct, every aspect of it necessary and dependent on every other aspect. Pull any bit out and it all collapses. The only choice being for everything to exist, or nothing to exist; no other options. There would be no way to edit reality down to just the lovely and pleasant bits. No power, no force, no God could do such.

In that case, the way to forgive the Universe for its shortcomings would be to recognize they are necessary and in service to the greater good/whole. The great price paid for existence would not be in vain but rather a testament to its great worth. For who would sacrifice all pleasure to do away with all suffering? Or eliminate all love to do away with all hate? This appears to be the predicament: The whole ball of wax or no ball of wax. It all comes down to whether you think it's worth the price.

The good hedonist forgives the Universe its shortcomings and embraces its treasures.

WHEN YOU CAN'T FORGIVE - ALTERNATIVES

If you're in a situation where you can't or don't want to forgive, then you can try other methods to release the negative emotions and find a certain amount of acceptance.

1. DILUTE. Our emotions seem small when compared to the totality of things. So put things in a greater context. Let's say I hate some asshole. If I imagine all the other assholes there are to hate, both now and in the past, it seems a bit pointless or silly to focus on one little douche. And to hate them all would be overwhelming and ridiculous. So letting go of the hate and releasing it out into the vastness of the cosmos seems a swell idea.

2. SEPARATE THOUGHT AND FEELING. Emotions have two components, thought and body sensation, which combine to create emotion. These can be separated, allowing one to retain the idea that, say, some person is an asshole worthy of hate, anger or resentment, yet release the feeling part of the emotion. One could be thinking "What an asshole" while feeling a comfortable acceptance. Not acceptance for the person or their actions, but accepting that the universe contains assholes and this particular person is one. Hate, anger and resentment are at war with that fact.

This is like the affirmation, "I can accept that assholes exist" which can apply to yourself as well as others.

3. PITY. Pity is a sort of halfway measure toward forgiveness and can ease negative emotions to some degree. It's fairly easy to muster, since most everyone we despise is pretty damn pitiful. I used it for many years to ease the hate I had for my stepfather; the stupid and pathetic jackass.

4. WHAT THE HELL. Fuck it. Just let it go. Life is too short and some emotions are just a pain in the ass. So release them back into the wild when you can: A "catch and release" program. You don't have to forgive to let go. This is a bit of a technical or semantic distinction but hey, fuck it, it works.

The good hedonist does their best to dissolve or release useless negative emotions.

16

FREEDOM AND THE ILLUSION OF FREE WILL

The existence of our individual free will is a sacred cow for many: a vital lynchpin in their world model. Some religious doctrines depend on it, crumbling into nonsense if it doesn't exist*. For many people it's the bulwark of their identity and sense of control, so undermining it appears to threaten their very existence. It's no wonder any questioning of this concept meets with a very determined opposition which has little interest in open-mindedly questioning the tightly held belief. After all, removing this keystone from their model of reality could bring the entire contraption down; which is no picnic. So go ahead and think I'm full of crap. Just please humor me a bit further.

Many assume if they don't have individual free will then everything must be fated or planned out, by God or whatever, and they would be mere puppets without any control or freedom. For some reason they see it as an either/or situation, but it's not. The lack of individual free will doesn't mean there must be something else calling the shots or planning your actions. Just as a rock can roll down a hill without a free will or a plan, so to

---

* Without the existence of our free will we can't be held accountable for our "sins". That creates a load of problems for many religious doctrines

you and the entire Universe can unfold.

What I presented in the last chapter is not that we have no will, but rather that our will itself is not what I'd call "free", because of the restrictive framework and limitations it operates within. It doesn't fit the sort of criteria that certain folks who champion the existence of our free will would need for their ideas of ultimate human responsibility to hold water. It fails that test hands down. But given another standard it could still be called "free" to some degree. It's not like it must be either completely free or completely not free. There's a lot of middle ground.

As far as I can tell, our will is simply a drive toward pleasure and away from suffering, operating much like magnetism, attracting and repulsing. Which would mean our decisions and actions aren't planned by our will any more than magnetism plans to make compass needles point north or gravity plans to hold us to the ground. It's our minds that create plans. Our will is expressed in our *feeling* about those plans. It's through feelings of acceptance or resistance that ideas get approval or disapproval, or are undecided with mixed or unclear feelings. The mind thinks, the will feels. The will can influence thoughts, but it isn't the source of them.

The planner/thinker and will are separate forces that combine in a very effective illusion that they are one. When we decide something, which is an act of will, it may appear to be a function of thinking but it's actually done through feeling.

But there's more to the picture. We also have subconscious thought processes and drives that generate feelings; strong feelings. Is that our will? Well, since

I've been driven nearly insane by some of those things, I'd say they aren't my will at all but rather a manipulation or imposition upon my will. The subconscious can be paranoid or defective in many ways, and our internal biological drives can be a terrible nuisance. To me these things feel like hijackers rather than my actual will.

In comparison, the basic will/drive toward pleasure and away from suffering is not an imposition or manipulation, but a *freedom* opening up a vast world of experience. Without it the Universe would be a much smaller place.

Our minds are wondrous things that have given us much. Mainly good but also bad. It can cause resistance to form in unlimited and complex ways that increase our suffering substantially. Of course it also gives us much greater abilities in seeking and increasing pleasure. The more your mind understands both those processes, the more it can serve your will. Which is the whole mission of this book.

IF A LEAF HAD A WILL

If a leaf had a will and fought the wind, it would feel like a prisoner and victim of that wind. If it willed to go with the wind, it would feel free. That basically is our situation. We have the power to feel free or feel imprisoned and victimized.

It's easy to see that the only real control the leaf has is in whether to resist reality or surrender and accept it. After all, a leaf can't get up and walk away. Though the leaf might feel in control of the wind when it happens to blow the way it wants, that would be an illusion.

Of course we have abilities a leaf doesn't. We can not only walk against the wind but build a plane and fly against it! But our powers to manipulate reality are still very limited. We can suffer and feel as powerless as the leaf in the wind. Then our situation is the same as the leaf's; fight reality and feel like a prisoner and victim, or surrender to reality and feel free.

Some might say the leaf is still a prisoner of the wind even if it feels otherwise, and that we're likewise always prisoners of reality no matter how we feel about it. But if the prison walls are built of only our own resistance, then removing that resistance actually does free oneself. After all, we are a part of reality, not a separate thing that could be imprisoned by it. The idea that we could be a prisoner of reality is only a concept existing in the mind. Reality is what we are; it allows us to exist. It is our freedom, not our jailer.

Never forget that we each are an intimate part of reality, the Universe and all there is. No matter how small, separate and insignificant we may seem, that is never the full size, scope or truth of who or what we are. Our actual borders are always beyond our comprehension, stretching deep into the unknown. And that is where our greatest freedom lies, in that unbound nature at the core of us and everything.

So, individual "free will" or not, freedom is ours. It's guaranteed by the mystery at the center of everything, which will always remain untamed and vital. It can never be completely explored, mapped, or known. No fences can enclose it, no boundaries can define it. And so it always remains unbound and free, raging eternally beyond our mind's grasp. Though we may map and bind and tame through our process of understanding and knowledge, our essential nature remains always free.

Since we've defined and packaged ourselves and our world to such an extreme degree, binding it up in our minds, we have a great need to reclaim our freedom and mystery. But we shouldn't enshrine freedom itself. Alone it's of no use and sometimes it's a source of suffering*. It's the dance between freedom and union that is of great value, because it is the fountain of such grand pleasures as love and bliss.

Strangely it's when we willingly surrender our personal freedom to that ultimate mystery that we become the most free. This is where the path of acceptance leads. Where our most intimate and vital parts are lain on the altar.

The good hedonist knows that true freedom is not achieved until you surrender your own.

---

*Our culture here in the USA stresses individual freedom so much that it can lead to feelings of alienation and being alone and adrift with little or no support or safety. Studies show the happiest countries are where the people feel the most taken care of and safe, even if they must give up some individual freedom and/or pay rather stiff taxes. Freedom from worry and fear is one of the most sought freedoms.

17

WHAT IS PLEASURE?

Ask a scientist what pleasure is and you might hear a lot about certain areas of the brain and various chemical neurotransmitters and such. But none those things are pleasure itself. Pleasure is an experience, not the physical structures and processes that may be involved in its creation. Just like music is not the physical objects and processes involved in its creation. One can map out and describe all the aspects of musical scores, musical instruments, sound waves, ears, nerves, brains, etc., yet music still must be heard and experienced to know what it actually is. Music, like pleasure, is an experience, and experience is a relationship between a consciousness and what it is conscious of.

The Universe is made of relationships. Even two simple points in space have certain basic relationships to one another. The distance between them. Whether they are moving toward or away from each other. Whether they are attracting or repelling each other. Things like that.

A feeling consciousness also has certain basic relationships to what it is conscious of. Two fundamental ones, which are the equivalent of the attraction or repulsion of two points, are acceptance and resistance. Pleasure is the felt experience of a relationship of acceptance. Suffering is the felt experience of a relationship of resistance. One is a relationship of harmony; the other a relationship of discord.

Everything we feel/experience exists on the stage of relationship. So, by simply adjusting your point of view, you are altering your relationship and thus altering your experience. It's a very simple dynamic that can have some very dramatic effects. Acceptance is a "point of view" that acts as a fulcrum with which we can lift our experienced world.

Acceptance is an action, a movement of opening. Much like the iris of an eye, the wider it opens the more light is let in, illuminating more harmony, union, and grandeur. It's an ever expanding miracle. This is pleasure. Not just a feeling, but a living truth.

Though we have a physical body in a physical universe, conscious experience is our home as well. And as vast and grand as the physical universe is, the internal universe may be even vaster and grander. Its range is immense. From the completely mundane to the colossally profound. From grotesque ugliness to sublime beauty. From unbearable suffering to ecstatic bliss. From total indifference to overwhelming love. From devastating isolation to joyous union with all. Conscious experience is a universe filled with many wonders, but it is pleasure which gives it value and makes it worthwhile.

Pleasure is not a mere mental or chemical gimmick born out of evolution that exists only to manipulate us. It's a fundamental truth as real as anything in the Universe. Evolution didn't invent it, but rather, used a natural principal that already existed. At least that's what I think makes more sense, and might explain why the scope of pleasure goes way beyond what's needed to fulfill the role of species' survival and propagation. That's a fact that doesn't quite fit the model of reality some in science have presented. While excuses and theories can be invented to explain it, they usually stink of a bias against considering any shift in one's already set beliefs*.

Pleasure is the light of the internal universe. It leads us from the darkest corners of existence to the grandly lit halls of ecstatic bliss and love. It provides us with value, meaning, and a reason to embrace existence. Without it we'd be absolutely lost.

The good hedonist knows the value of pleasure and lets it light the way.

---

* It's natural to cling to one's model of reality because it provides a feeling of stability and security. But find some balls!

18

WHAT IS THE ULTIMATE PLEASURE?

Some might interpret that question to mean what activity brings the greatest pleasure, but that's not what I mean at all. Activities are just a means to acquire pleasure, they aren't pleasure itself. Sex, drugs, sky diving, scrabble; whatever gets you off may not the next person. Pleasure, like beauty, only exists in the beholder.

So let me restate the question. What is the ultimate *state* of pleasure?

We have words such as "rapture", "ecstasy", and "bliss" for states of great pleasure, but they only advance the question to "What is the ultimate state of rapture, ecstasy or bliss?" To be more specific from there one usually has to resort to, and get mired in, various eastern religious or "spiritual" terms and concepts (nirvana, samadhi, etc.) for certain advanced states of consciousness, perception or being. Basically they all mean some sort of liberation, enlightenment, or union with "God" or the cosmos. They are all supposed to be incredibly pleasurable, if not the ultimate pleasure then something very close to it. However, since the terms come from various religious traditions, and we know that religions have a history of making wild claims, it's wise to view these terms with a certain amount of suspicion. It's also probably safe to say these states do actually exist in some form or another. They may not be exactly what they are claimed to be, but enough people from all beliefs (or non-beliefs) and walks of life have had these kinds of experiences (as interpreted through their own beliefs and biases) to conclude they are not just complete hyperbole or bullshit. After all, one could drop the fancy exotic labels and simply call them grand states of rapture, ecstasy, and bliss. The important aspect is that all who've experienced them feel those moments were the most pleasurable or fulfilling they've ever experienced.

Whatever you think these experiences actually are, the case for the ultimate pleasure being out in their neck of the woods is fairly solid. But don't assume that these sorts of experiences *cause* great pleasure. It may be the other way around. Or that they rise together, two halves of one thing.

Invariably, anyone experiencing truly grand states of pleasure feels there is something otherworldly and transcendent about it. It's not just pleasurable, it's profound, moving, and meaningful. The feeling that you are touching something much greater than yourself, or are a breath away from some sort of enlightenment or grand truth, is inescapable once pleasure reaches a certain level. This is the case no matter what your beliefs, biases, and prejudices. Something happens in the upper reaches of pleasure where it takes on more dimensions and qualities, becoming something so grand that people must use grander terms and concepts to describe it. Great pleasure is something much more complex and interesting than pleasure as we normally think of it. It's not simply a larger version of the same thing, but more like a doorway, the wider it's opened the more that can come through.

As I see it, acceptance, the fundamental principal behind pleasure, has a natural inclination to open up, draw together, connect, and unify. On the other hand, resistance has the natural inclination to close up, push apart, disconnect, and separate. So the natural progression as one moves from the constricting and isolating confines of resistance and suffering, and toward increasing amounts of acceptance and pleasure, is that one's world opens up, connects and deepens more and more. This is the movement of acceptance, and as it increases your world expands. Its size, dimensions, depth, unity and qualities increase and expand. And that expansion could be called "enlightenment", even if it's only an enlightenment of the realm of internal experience.

BUT WHAT ABOUT JUNKIES AND SADISTS?

I'm saying pleasure, acceptance, and "enlightenment" are fundamentally linked, if not all aspects of one thing. But there is a good argument against that idea: the fact that there are some who get pleasure from things such as cruelty or heroin, which don't appear to promote "enlightenment" in any way, shape or form! That would seem to prove pleasure must be independent from any sort of enlightenment, but it doesn't. You have to keep in mind that a state of 1% enlightenment is still 99% darkness, so it can be present in some small way but completely lost in the vast ocean of its opposite. And some pleasure is just a momentary lessening of suffering resulting from the temporary loosening of some base tension or psychological thumbscrew.

Repeated loosening and tightening of that thumbscrew can milk out bits of pleasure, acceptance and rudimentary "enlightenment" over and over without any net gain. It's just a speck in an ocean of shit. It bobs to the surface for a moment and then disappears.

IF ENLIGHTENMENT WAS A BORE

"Enlightenment" more literally means being in a state of *understanding*, free of ignorance. In the context of these "higher" states it doesn't mean mental knowledge but rather seeing/experiencing reality clearly and fully as it truly is, rather than seeing/experiencing an illusion or mental construct. That's the conceit at least, which if true sounds good, but what if reality was actually a hideous abomination that if seen clearly would make you completely miserable? Or what if it were a huge bore? Or just not so great? Wouldn't spiritual enlightenment be a grand disappointment if it wasn't profoundly and deeply pleasurable? Isn't pleasure an essential quality that gives value to all these elevated states? What would they be without it?*

There are many in spiritual and religious circles that prefer to see these states as primarily about something more respectable than pleasure. They need to open their

---

*I've heard of "enlightenment" experiences that weren't very pleasurable, but they are almost always had by folks tripping on some drug and the experiences are always very bizarre, like churned out by a demented sci-fi writer on a speed bender. These don't qualify as the sort of state I'm referring to.

There's also the argument that unpleasant "ego-death" experiences are enlightenment experiences, but by definition they are about illusion and resistance. What might follow them is another issue.

eyes to the fact that pleasure is what gives value to all those more "respectable" things. Even the very concept of respectability couldn't exist without pleasure. Pleasure is eminently respectable and fundamentally fused to every good thing. And all these grand states of consciousness seem to shout its most exalted position.

For those that believe in a creator type God, ask yourself why God created everything? The inescapable answer is for "his" own pleasure. If pleasure is the motivation for even God, then it should be obvious that pleasure's station in things is exalted beyond anything we can conceive.

Pleasure isn't just a side effect of these "enlightened" states but an integral part of them. It is the living experience of acceptance and the unity it provides. Without acceptance these states can't be accessed. At best they could only be glimpsed from the point of view of an alienated outsider, which is a false perception. Pleasure is the needed component to remove the walls of separation.

While I can't say I've personally ever experienced anything so grand as "enlightenment" or "liberation" for even a tiny moment, I can say the greatest pleasures I've ever experienced were also the greatest experiences of enlightenment, liberation, love, or contact with "God" I've ever experienced. For me the relationship of pleasure to those things is too intimately fused to separate. They are the same thing.

Call the experiences what you will, or declare me delusional. Until you have personally felt such experiences I can't really blame you. Describe them to someone who hasn't had such and you may as well be talking about Moon-men eating Moon-cheese. I can't expect everyone to relate to it, only those that have been there to some degree.

As for those that have been far beyond anything I've experienced, I concede my ignorance. But if you think you are "enlightened", I apologize for my skepticism but there's a crap-load of you folks around and most are fucking idiots. Of course there's bound to be more phonies, crazies, and deluded than the real deal, but even the very most impressive can't prove they are truly enlightened, or if such is even possible. States of "knowing" are often delusional, but pleasure is always real. Ultimately it's pleasure that provides the obvious and undeniable value to any "enlightened" state, whether that state is real or delusional.

DIY NIRVANA

One outcome of this pleasure-centric view is it places these "higher" type experiences into the hands of everyone. Not reserved for just the very pure, saintly, dedicated, persevering, knowledgeable, enlightened, faithful, austere, or extreme "true believers". In other words it takes it out of the domain of religion and rarefied esoteric spiritual practices, and into the hands of everyone, where it belongs. No more a spiritual stunt of the religious or "spiritual" elite: this is DIY nirvana for everyone.

If the ultimate truth and the ultimate pleasure are one, then the good hedonist and the seeker of truth are also one.

REEL IT IN, KNUCKLEHEAD!

Okay, I don't want anyone to head in the wrong direction, so allow me to offer the following.

1. Please don't get the idea that any impulse you have for pleasure is also a step on the path to enlightenment! Much of our impulses are driven by our resistance and desire to escape suffering. If your "pleasure" is really about blocking, masking or avoiding pain/suffering, it's probably headed in the wrong direction. To be in a state of resistance and try to manipulate yourself into a state of acceptance through the use of drugs, food, sex, power trips, shopping, bank heists, etc., is an act of avoidance, grasping, force, that may actually give your resistance more power. As a control trip it leads away from acceptance and toward a manipulative relationship with the Universe. By artificially forcing temporary acceptance, one creates a dependence which robs them of their true inner power to dissolve resistance and create pleasure.

2. It's a mistake to have a goal of attaining the *ultimate pleasure* or grand states of enlightenment, liberation, etc. First off, when you have grand goals it can create grand disappointments, because anything less than achieving them becomes something of a failure.

And secondly, there's the problem inherent in the process of wanting, which declares that the present moment is lacking and so blocks acceptance and adds to one's resistance and suffering. You can't accept or embrace the moment if you're seeing it as lacking and are focused on some far off grand desire/goal.

To want the ultimate pleasure, or other grand states of consciousness, is an obstacle to attaining them. The approach is rather though the humility of acceptance, not the ego-driven drive to achieve, or the anxiety/fear driven drive to obtain, escape or control. It's not something you grab hold of. It's something you can find only by letting go.

For the good hedonist the ultimate pleasure is not the goal, but rather to just be able to find the pleasure inherent in each moment.

There exists a state so deeply satisfying that all desires are extinguished in its wake; from this vantage point any greater pleasure is pointless and holds no power over you. It's a place that is profoundly enough, and not very far from wherever you are. But it's never found by striving for it.

The goal of the good hedonist is not far off or
difficult to obtain, it can be had in any moment.

19

THE MAGICAL CARPET STAIN

Just because someone has an experience that feels profound or meaningful, or thinks it some sort of enlightenment, touch of God, or whatever, that doesn't exactly prove it to be so. We can be fooled fairly easily and are wrong often. So what is the truth of these grandly pleasurable experiences that feel so loaded with profound truth? Are they what they seem to be or mere illusions farted out by our brains?

To explore this let's take a look at a very bland and uninteresting experience: looking at an ordinary stain on an ordinary carpet. Most everyone would see it as just that, an ordinary stain on an ordinary carpet, ugly and uninteresting. But what if there's a person who sees it as a thing of beauty and wonder, infused with deep profoundness? Is that person delusional or are the others? Which of them is seeing reality the most accurately?

Obviously, most will go along with the majority on this. But what exactly is the true and complete reality of that carpet stain and what would it be like to actually see it in total? Imagine clearly seeing all the facets of its atomic and subatomic structure, and all the laws of physics acting upon it. The dance of electrons, the vibration of the atoms, the traveling photons bouncing off it, and it's full connection and place within the greater universe. That humble little stain's matter would have a long history stretching all the way back to the Big Bang (or whatever)! Billions of years of history all packed into that stain! Seeing all that would blow anyone away. It would most likely appear beautiful, wondrous and profound. But there's even more to it than that. To be seen at all there must be a consciousness viewing it, which adds a whole other level of profound mystery and wonder.

So, considering all that, which person was seeing reality the most accurately?

The real question here is about feeling, not seeing. Everyone sees the same pattern of stain on carpet (sort of). No one is actually seeing the subatomic structure or history of the stain's matter. But it turns out the more extraordinary *feelings* about the stain are more in line with the reality/truth/facts than the opposite is. The bland, boring stain is more of an illusion than the wondrous one.

While it truly is just an ordinary stain, our normal way of seeing ordinary things is far removed from a complete picture of reality. Limitations of our senses and the way our minds create a simplified and more practical version or mock-up of reality see to that. Ordinary daily reality is profoundly more extraordinary than how we normally perceive it. And although it's impossible to quantify exactly what "reality" is*, it's not a stretch to say it's extraordinarily dynamic, energetic, powerful, connected, complete, and we are part of it. All of these are profoundly experienced in grandly pleasurable states, but lacking in more ordinary states. And states of suffering, even the most "dynamic" and

---

*While we know lots of details, there are always questions beyond our ability to answer. Mystery will always be a big part of reality.

"powerful", always require an amount of separation and incompleteness.

Our minds are great at creating illusions, so I'm not saying the grand perceptions that accompany our highest states of pleasure are necessarily visions of reality itself, just that these states have a greater affinity to reality than other experiential states. What to make of that is up to you.

The revelation of the good hedonist is that pleasure has a greater affinity to truth and reality than suffering.

20

PUNK MYSTIC

When the hedonist ventures out beyond ordinary pleasures to the realms of transcendental bliss and ecstasy, he/she enters the domain of the mystic.

This is my tale of youth, when I was a DIY punk mystic, naively raiding the treasure.

I was raised an atheist. It was basic "the Bible is stupid nonsense" sort of atheism. Attacking tales of arks in floods and men swallowed by whales. All the easy targets. It made perfect sense. Religion was dumb. And when you're dead, you're dead.

As a teenager I started finding out there was more to religion than just stupid old tales that were plainly fiction. It was the late 60's and eastern religions were getting more exposure in the west. On the radio I'd hear talks by Ram Das (Richard Albert). On TV (UHF) I saw old shows Alan Watts did about Zen Buddhism. And I was reading books on Eastern religion and various Gurus. It all made religion, even Christianity, more interesting. I was opening my mind more to possibilities and at some point decided I was an agnostic.

In the midst of all that, something very interesting happened. On a whim, but sincerely and humbly, I decided to invite "God" into my heart just to see if anything would happen. It was just an experiment to which I had low expectations of anything interesting resulting. To my utter surprise I had a profound experience that completely blew me away and changed my universe permanently. There were no visions or voices, just an overwhelmingly profound feeling that I was in contact with something uniquely powerful, deeply moving, and wonderful. It filled me to overflowing with a contentment, depth, and majesty I had never known.

It lasted only a minute or two and I wasn't really sure what exactly to make of it. I knew it was the sort of experience that might cause some to embrace a religion. If this experience happened while, say, some preacher laid his hands on me, or I chanted some "holy" name, I could see how I might take it as a powerful affirmation or proof. Since the idea to ask God into my heart came mainly from Christians, it did cross my mind I might have just been "born again", but the experience itself seemed very nondenominational with no undertone or overtone supporting any particular religion whatsoever. I felt I had contact with something one might call "God", but it left me with the distinct impression "God" was completely free and separate from religion or any concept of what God was. "God" was simply way beyond any of them. So the experience didn't drive me toward any particular religion. If I was "born again", it was into the "spirit", not into a religion.

For me the most important thing about the experience was it revealed the universe to be a much more interesting place than I had previously known or imagined. Because at the very least I now knew there were realms of experience way beyond anything I had ever dealt with or conceived of, with much greater depth, beauty, pleasure, and promise. It was like a door opened to a new world and I wanted to explore those realms, whatever they were. It was the most interesting thing I'd ever encountered and it left me with a reverence I hold to this day.

After that I explored those realms as best I could. I read and listening to various "teachers" but followed none. I made up my own way, feeling free to use what I liked, discard what I didn't, developing my own beliefs and methods of meditation. It was do-it-yourself mysticism by a young punk who made his own rules. Amazingly, it worked quite well for many years. I got by on innocence and the reverence and humility my first encounter had given me. Eventually I was able to enter states of relative bliss nearly at will. I didn't see myself as a hedonist back then, but I sure was awash in sublime pleasure.

Innocence can last only so long. My end came when I slowly became too involved with a certain religion, which happened mainly by happenstance. Its belief system slowly crept in, influencing and infecting my own at a pace too gradual to notice. It left me exposed to the weaknesses and flaws of that religion, which were apparent to me from the beginning yet I still got sucked in. Not fully in, as there was plenty I never bought into, but enough to leave me vulnerable.

By the time I noticed what was happening and left the influence of that religion, it was too late. I thought I could just go back to what I had before on my own, but that was not the case. I had a collapse of faith, and my bliss-fest was MIA.

It's a very curious thing; I lost much of my ability to experience pleasure. Perhaps being used to so much bliss made anything less feel like nearly nothing, but there was more to it than just that. It's not easy to fully describe, even my perceptions were effected. Distant things like hills or mountains took on a strange quality where they appeared to be made of cardboard. It's not that they actually looked any different, they just *felt* different.

It took me quite a while to figure out why that might be. I think it's about one's mental model of reality, which fleshes out the world we each see. My loss of faith messed with that model enough that mountains lost the weight and substance my mind had formally filled them with. So they felt like empty cardboard shells.

Beliefs, models, concepts can become so entwined and interdependent that pulling out one bit can bring down many others with it. This sort of damage is not so easy to fix or heal. After all, your mental model of the world is built from all your years of experience. Brick by brick. You can't replace that overnight. And I certainly couldn't.

It took a full two years before I felt anything close to normal. But what I wanted was not just to be merely "normal" but back to where I once was, diving in fountains of bliss. Fact is I had been spoiled and things just didn't measure up; which created an endless amount of resistance, making my universe into a prison.

Navigating that resistance is what eventually led to this book. To find my way I had to strip everything down to the bare bones, challenging every belief and concept no matter how dear. Not once but many times. It's been a long and difficult road, winding over 30 years. I've had to constantly redefine, toss out, alter, strip down and rebuild. Whenever I thought I had a good handle on things, some event would come along and prove I didn't. Make progress, fall back, repeat. Everything together becoming the forge hammering out the ideas you see here. No matter how full of shit you may think I am, please understand this "shit" was hard earned and is sincere.

Hedonism is the unadorned path, stripped of all pretense, myth and bullshit. Yet rather than destroying mystery it instead leads deeply into it. Just as you can't sky dive without eventually reaching the ground, so too you can't follow pleasure without eventually having to embrace the fundamental mystery which is at the heart of reality and is the very ground of our being. That is why this unadorned path of the mere hedonist ends up treading the same rarified ground as the mystic, where bliss abides in every atom.

While it may seem to many an improper path, good for only lowly scalawags and uncouth punks, it is in truth the purest and straightest, forged in our very being, uniting us with everything.

The good hedonist's embrace of pleasure ultimately leads to embracing the mystery of existing.

21

THE PLEASURE MACHINE

I hate to disappoint you but there is no actual physical "pleasure machine". The "Orgasmatron" has not yet been invented. What I'm actually referring to is meditation. A let down, I know. Sorry. But please hear me out.

For many, meditation is about as welcome an idea as going to the dentist or unclogging a toilet. They may see it as difficult, unpleasant, awkward or boring. Like one of those unpleasant tasks that is supposed to be good for you but is excruciatingly dull. Or perhaps they think it's lame crap for religious nuts, sissies, and weirdos. Meditation is saddled with an aura of foreign strangeness, corny new-age silliness, and un-masculine dorkiness. And even if you have no negative feelings about it, you probably feel you have no time for it.

Altogether that's a lot working against it; which is too bad, because it's one of the greatest tools available for decreasing resistance and increasing acceptance. And if you've been paying attention you know that means it can function as a quite effective pleasure generator. So the good hedonist should try to overcome whatever bullshit may be in the way and embrace meditation, adapting it to their goals.

Meditation was first introduced to me as a spiritual pursuit one does to become more enlightened (or whatever you wish to call it). This may seem far removed from being a "pleasure generator" but the only reason anyone seeks enlightenment or pursues spiritual goals is because of the underlying assumption it will in some way lead to higher and more fulfilling states of enjoyment. Plus, as I already covered (in Chapter 18), I would argue that enlightenment itself is an advanced state of pleasure. So there actually is a common purpose between the spiritual seeker and the good hedonist, whether they know it or not, and meditation can serve both equally.

Of course nowadays meditation is also commonly used for practical secular purposes, such as to ease stress or promote relaxation and mental or physical health. Which sounds pretty dull and boring compared to enlightenment, but those goals are exceedingly more sane and completely in line with the good hedonist's aims.

Adapting meditation methods from either camp is not difficult. Some are already good-to-go, or close to it. Many Buddhist methods are particularly well suited*, but whatever works for you is what matters. Feel free to alter, take a bit from one and a bit from another, or invent your own methods.

At first it will take some trial and error experimenting. No doubt some methods and practices will not be your cup of tea. Don't let that discourage you! I hated and rejected the majority of the most well-known and popular methods and practices - such as closing your eyes or following your breath - yet still eventually found, created or developed things that worked well for

---

* Shinzen Young is one source (check youtube). I originally heard him on the radio and appropriated some very useful concepts. A few appear mangled in this book, but don't blame him!

me.

Keep in mind that the standard image of closed eyes, sitting alone cross-legged in a quiet peaceful place, is just a stereotype. You can meditate eyes wide open in the middle of a riot too. Or while running, eating, talking, standing in line at the Post Office, watching TV, playing Whack-A-Mole, whatever. Anytime, anywhere. Although beginners should probably go for the "quiet peaceful place" until they get familiar with the process.

Don't think of meditation as something unnatural you must force yourself to do. It's actually something you already do naturally. Anytime you consciously focus your attention, you are meditating. It's as simple as that. Be it on TV, food, sex, thoughts, emotions, work, actions, sensations, pain, pleasure, a sunset, a book, music, prayer, Porky Pig, an assault rifle, tiddlywinks, the moment, or your own consciousness. Proper meditation just gets you to be more aware of it, refine it, strengthen it, and direct it in certain ways.

Developing personalized techniques that work for you can't form overnight, so have patience. Once they do form they can become a nearly effortless habit that may subtly or overtly carry over into nearly every waking moment.

Meditation is an exploration of self and reality. If you're comfortable with those things you should be comfortable with meditation. If not you'll have some difficulty, but that difficulty points to the very issues you need to work on, because we all wish to be comfortable with ourselves and reality.

For the good hedonist the focus can simply be on dissolving resistance and increasing acceptance. It need not get any more complicated than that. While that may sound simple and boring, I assure you that in practice it's not. If you consider that releasing tension is essentially what an orgasm is, you may get the point. The releasing or dissolving of deep pockets of subtle tension or resistance, and the expansion and deepening of acceptance, can be very pleasurable and absorbing. Very! And it can lead to transcending the confining boarders of one's self image and world model, sending one out into rich landscapes of bliss. It truly can be a pleasure machine.

DISCLAIMER - I should state here that I'm certainly no meditation expert or teacher. So I'm not going to be giving any detailed "how to" instructions. But I will try to describe some of the ways I now use meditation and how I think it works.

What I usually use now has four basic themes or flavors:

1. First is I focus on any physical kernel or pool of acceptance in myself and try to expand it. This will only work if you can find that kernel or pool, but once you're familiar with what to look for it's usually not difficult. And by that I don't mean mentally ruminating, I mean looking within for a physical sensation of acceptance. Though a thought may be there, the focus is on the physical sensation of acceptance (or see it as non-resistance, letting go, whatever). Expanding that will feel like a pleasurable opening up or release.

When I first began meditating I saw it as "opening the heart". That was the conceptual hook I used at the time, because it resonated with me. Only much later did I start seeing it as "increasing acceptance". You may need to find your own conceptual hook that works for you. Whatever encourages, expands, or deepens acceptance will do. Anything from "fuck it" to something more religious or spiritual. "Loving God" or any sort of reverence, submitting or merging with God, the Universe, or "higher power", might be the acceptance expanding key for you personally. What I've done for myself, out of personal necessity, is strip it down to its essence, which is *acceptance*. Whatever works for you is up to you to find out. And it may change over time.

2. Second, if no acceptance is present then I use any physical tension or resistance in myself at that moment and focus on releasing or dissolving it. Again, no mental ruminating, just focusing on the physical sensation of it. Learning to see and then release or dissolve resistance will take practice. At first you may feel blind, not knowing exactly what to look for or where. Just understand that if you aren't in a perfectly content state, then you have resistance somewhere. Try looking in the same place you would normally feel joy or love. Is any tension, constriction, hollowness, anxiety, fear, or uncomfortable feelings there? They might be very subtle and "under the radar", which is why it takes the focus of meditation to find and deal with them.

Once you locate resistance, don't attempt to fight it or try pushing it away! Just identify it as resistance and try to bring some acceptance to it. It's dissolved, or broken up, by opening it up, not by confronting or restricting it (which is just more resistance). This is another skill that will develop over time. As tension or resistance is released, pleasure and acceptance is produced. Conceptually you will probably focus on the "event horizon", were the one transforms into the other.

3. Third is I focus on any neutral body sensation. I usually use skin surface sensation or general body tension/sense (others often use breath) and observe it with as much absorption and equanimity as I can manage. By "equanimity" I mean to observe it as you would something outside yourself, without judgment. Just like watching a cloud roll by, not identifying with it as part of yourself.

Our feeling of self and ego is constructed from body sensations, mental concepts/images, and the sensation of thinking. These components congeal into what appears to be one thing, yourself. But it's not really one thing or you. So if you focus on just body sensation and allow yourself to experience it as you would something outside yourself (in other words don't identify with it) then it can move from being a part of that construct into being something free-floating and separate (perhaps like a vibrating force). That dissolves the self-image enough to allow you to expand beyond that boundary. So rather than a defined ego encased in a physical body, you feel more like undefined free-floating consciousness. Which may not sound so hot as you read this but the actual experience should prove to be liberating and pleasurable; effectively dissolving a source of resistance and expanding acceptance.

The intellectualizing above is not part of the process and might be a distraction, so remember to keep the focus mainly on the physical sensation, not mental stuff.

4. Fourth is I focus on anything outside of myself, such as what I'm looking at. I bring as much concentration, equanimity, and absorption to that as I can muster. This requires a lack of resistance within, so it seems to naturally draw me into a state of acceptance and loosen the boundaries of "self" and world.

I DON'T THINK, THEREFORE I'M WHAT?

Becoming less identified with your thoughts is also liberating, being as it's another part of the ego construct. However, most of us are really stuck on that one, so it's much trickier to work with in meditation than body sensations. It can be done, but it probably would be best to not drive yourself nuts on it right off. Just understand that your mind can generate thoughts much like a machine and you shouldn't feel responsible for all the crap it's churning out. At times it can be very helpful to see a thought as "just a thought" and not something you must give any weight to or take any responsibility for. You aren't the thought machine. It's just a tool we're very attached to and intimate with.

Early on, when I first began meditating, I had heard something about stopping thinking, so I put a lot of effort into it. At first it seemed impossible but soon I found some success in just slowing my thoughts down to a crawl until they'd seem to stop momentarily. That felt pretty interesting and became a very useful trick that I used in meditation so much it became second nature. I often forget it's still a major part of what I'm doing, and it's hard for me to judge its importance because I can't remember what it was like beforehand. It's been a long time.

Of course by "stopping thinking" I just mean the words. There's still a level of thinking that goes on that doesn't use words, and there's subconscious thinking, so you're not really stopping all thinking, just stopping the mental flow of words. This helps release you from feeling that you live in your skull churning out words. As the words stop, you expand outward and move from being a thinker to being a consciousness with a less defined center or boundary.

I don't want to give the impression that thoughts are something only to be repressed in meditation. I've used them a lot in the past to great effect, and still do. Writing this book took a lot of meditation on thoughts; or more precisely, on concepts. But I don't mean you're just sitting there thinking about a concept. I mean you are completely focused on seeing and feeling that concept as a living reality you exist within, and you stay right there awhile. That can be very interesting and fruitful. But the "stay right there awhile" part is tricky and involves being able to do what I mentioned above, slowing down thinking to a crawl. Holding focus on a thought/concept takes the same skill, or else other thoughts would just push it aside.

As I already said, I'm not a meditation teacher. My only experience is with myself. For me, slowing my thinking is the same as slowing talking. Simple, but if I remember right it wasn't all that simple at first. Sorry to say that's all I remember or can offer about it.

GROUPS, TEACHERS AND ASSHOLES

Group meditation is a big turn-off for me. It seems ridiculous to gather in a group just to completely ignore each other. Why? Is it to show off, or out of some sort of insecurity? What's the draw? A group is a huge distraction, so not good for meditation at all.

I'm kidding a bit there, I know some require the structure and discipline. And obviously many go for direct access to a meditation teacher they can ask questions of and get personal instruction. You can't do that with writings or recordings.

The thing to always keep in mind is that all teachers and groups have some sort of reality model and bias, whether it's overt or hidden. This could be a danger, especially to the easily influenced. So be selective and careful, since I assume your goal is not to join a religion or cult. Don't ever be seduced by airs of spiritual superiority. It's always bullshit.

Rule of thumb - Anyone presenting themselves as anything other than a regular human being is not to be trusted. And any group presenting themselves as having ultimate knowledge is not to be trusted. And all persons presenting themselves as being "spiritual" are just as fucked-up as the rest of us (if not more).

THE FOG OF FAMILIARITY AND THE PRISON OF KNOWING

Familiarity can make the present moment appear to be dull and uninteresting. It's our mind's habit of prioritizing: paying more attention to novelty or things that may be a danger or have some particular use to our needs, desires and demands. It's survival strategy. Regular stuff gets simplified, dulled, glossed over and taken for granted, so you can better focus on what your instincts feel matters most. This develops a habit of seeing things in certain ways, which can become something of a prison; creating boredom and making the world appear dull, unappealing, or worse. Meditation can break down those walls, overcoming the habits of the mind, allowing things to appear more fresh, beautiful, and interesting. It can loosen or dissolve the mental boundaries, images, models, and beliefs that fog and limit our vision of the world, thus allowing one to venture beyond the restrictive, default, pieced-together model of reality that's accumulated over the years, and out into vast new untamed territories. The domesticated Universe is breached.

LET'S NOT OVER-HYPE IT

I don't wish to over-hype meditation. Though it can be very helpful, it's not like it's a panacea and if you just do it enough you'll be a great hedonist or become "enlightened" in some way. Someone could meditate their whole life and still remain a total idiot douche bag. And it can be used and abused in negative ways. I'm sure meditation addicts exist, wasting their lives away in self-imposed meditation exile, chasing their desire for enlightenment and attempting to force the Universe to comply to their grand demands and delusions. But since the good hedonist isn't looking for something so grand as enlightenment but rather just the practical matter to enjoy more and suffer less, the danger of anything negative from it is minimal.

Meditation can help decipher the mechanics of how suffering and pleasure are created within us, giving one much more control over the process. So it's an important tool for the good hedonist to make use of.

The good hedonist recognizes the value of meditation in becoming a skilled hedonist.

22

LOVE IS NOT DESIRE

Love is enshrined in our culture, yet there's a lot of confusion about what it actually is. It doesn't help that the word is commonly used to mean various things, or that science flounders about with chemical descriptions. But it's very important for the good hedonist to understand both what love is and is not. This can help one avoid much unnecessary suffering, and increase enjoyment exponentially.

Most everyone understands that the term "making love" is just a euphemism for sexual activity, and that love is actually something quite different than sexual attraction, passion or lust. Yet many are still fooled by feelings of sexual attraction and desire into thinking they are "in love". The problem isn't so much that they don't know there's a difference between lust and love, but rather that they confuse *desire* with love, which is a very common mistake. People just have a hard time, in certain situations, distinguishing love from intense want. Especially when love and want become so entangled it's hard to see where one leaves off and the other begins.

The entanglement is largely because we desire love so much. Love not only offers grand pleasures but also may seem a solution to various sufferings and issues. What better salve is there for insecurity and loneliness? What better validation to a wounded or alienated ego?

What better tonic for the sad and miserable? Love is often the envisioned cure-all for whatever ails you, and that is how desire drives its hooks deep into love. Well, that and the whole sex thing, of course.

If one is ever going to understand what love is they must disentangle it from desire. So let me stress the point - DESIRE IS NOT LOVE. Just because you want someone badly doesn't mean you love them. Wanting or craving someone intensely isn't love; it's just intense desire, want or demand - which is the real source of all suffering blamed on love. The term "love sick" really means "desire sick".

And if you're excited and elated about some person, that's not love either. It's just excitement and elation coming from the anticipation that your desires are being fulfilled.

The confusion is such that the term "in love" can mean a state that has no actual love involved at all. Though "in love" can at times mean a state of real love, it's more commonly used to mean one is in the grip of very strong desires, attraction, anticipation, and craving for another person. It's a very biologically driven state, where one's body floods with various mood altering chemicals; nature trying to get you to mate up. This is the sort of "love" scientists often study, since it's chemical components lend themselves so handily to measurement and simple answers. But I don't consider this love at all. It's just your desires and body messing with you. That's why I draw a very hard line between "in love" and love, as two very different and distinct things. So understand that when I use the term "in love" I mean this state of heightened desire, craving, attraction and anticipation; which isn't love at all.

Being "in love" can be very pleasant or pure torture. It's nature's carrot and stick, creating pleasant sensations or unpleasant, as is needed in its scheme to form a successfully breeding pair. I know it's not a very pretty or romantic picture! What can I say? Nature is what it is, and it's not all roses and rainbows.

LOVE IS NOT A DEMAND

Whether it's real love or "in love", both can be a nucleus that desires and demands form around. Usually a truck load of them! So apply everything I said in previous chapters about desires and demands.

Trying to sort them all out might be near impossible, but love itself can be separated from the mess. One way to distinguish actual love is it's always pleasurable. Always. You might think otherwise but all pain blamed on love actually comes from other sources. For instance, if the one you love dumps you, or even dies, the pain you feel doesn't come directly from your love but rather from your desire or demand for that person to not leave you. This may be about your desire/demand for love itself, or to not be alone, etc., etc. There could be hundreds of them.

Some might say it comes from your "attachment" to the other person, but I think that's an imprecise way to put it which can be misleading and at times damaging. Especially in the way some Buddhists, or faux Buddhists, commonly use it, where the implication is one should be non-attached. The problem with that is it seems to be saying one should strip themselves of all their emotional attachments, which would be asinine. You only need to strip yourself of troublesome demands, which are negative attachments. To strip yourself of positive attachments, like love, would be a crime.

Of course it's only a misunderstanding. I'm sure Buddhists talking about non-attachment don't mean to strip yourself of love! I'm no expert but I assume they just mean one should be non-grasping, non-demanding, non-resisting, and accepting. In other words; not harboring demands.

So, a person losing a loved one doesn't need to break their attachment, which is impossible anyway, but rather to accept that their loved one is gone though they deeply wish it were otherwise. You don't dissolve your attachment to them, you dissolve your demand. There may always be some resistance to them being gone, but if enough acceptance is brought to the situation it doesn't have to create suffering. That's not to say the goal in this sort of case would be to eliminate all the suffering, a certain amount may stand testament to the value one feels for the lost loved one, and in that has its own worth.

We have lots of desires and demands that tightly attach to love because love is so pleasurable and valued. Everyone wants it and no one wants to lose it. And in one's confusion about what love actually is, it can appear to be very illusive and beyond one's power. This can make you feel weak, vulnerable, frustrated, and despairing. But if you understand what love is and how desires attach to it, you see the situation is really not so dire. To be able to focus on just love itself, letting all the attached desires float away, is a liberation.

For the good hedonist it's essential to be able to

distinguish love from all it's not: Both to deal with or avoid suffering, and to discover greater pleasure and fulfillment.

LOVE AT FIRST SIGHT?

Sometimes it's the *idea* you hold of a person that you love, not the actual person. Only after you get to know a person well can you be sure that's not what's going on.

UNCONDITIONAL LOVE

Love that depends on certain conditions being met is conditional love. You love them because they fulfill, or you believe they will fulfill, certain desires you hold. Unconditional love has no dependence on conditions being met. None of your desires or demands must be met by the other person for you to love them. It's usually very difficult to tell if you have this sort love, unless you lose all hope that person will fulfill any of your desires; which can be a very unpleasant and trying situation! After all, these are most likely your deepest desires that reside in your most vulnerable and tender spots. The connections between love and our desires go very, very deep.

SO, WHAT THE HELL IS IT?

I've said a lot about what love isn't, now I guess I'd better say what it is! Turns out that's the harder task. While I personally have a very clear perception of what I believe it is, it's not so easy to convey to others or find agreement. As an experiment I decided to play a little word game to figure out what is the essential nature of love. I took all the words used to describe love in a typical dictionary definition, then strained and distilled them down to an essence, to see where it would lead.

Here's how it went.

The dictionaries I had said love can mean feelings of, desire, deep tender affection, strong attraction (sexual or otherwise), deep devotion, great fondness, great interest, passionate interest, sexual passion, deep attachment, to cherish, great appreciation, to adore, to greatly value, and to greatly care about. Keep in mind the dictionary is only stating the meaning of the various ways the word is commonly used, not giving the definitive meaning of what love itself actually is.

First I threw out sexual attraction and passion, being as everyone agrees those aren't love.

Next I tested each remaining word by asking if it's possible to have a great amount of that particular thing yet not any love. If the answer was yes, then I eliminated it. If the answer was no, then the word was kept and should have some close correlation with what love actually is.

Here's a rundown of the words that failed to measure up, done two or three at a time.

One may deeply desire and be extremely attracted to someone yet not love them at all.

One may be very attached and devoted to a job but have no love for it.

One may greatly value and have extreme interested and passion for a big stash of gold but not love it at all.

One may deeply appreciate and care greatly about their home but not love it.

Words that failed the test then are: desire, attraction, passion, devotion, interest, attachment, care, appreciation and value.

"Adore" had to go too because it can mean either to "love greatly" or "honor highly". The first is redundant and "honor" fails the test. The root of the word means "to worship". Worship fails too.

Words that passed are: affection, fondness and cherish. It's my opinion you couldn't have a great amount of any one of those without there being love present.

Fondness is affection, so it's redundant and can be eliminated. So we're left with just "cherish" and "affection".

Cherish is "to hold dear or feel love for". Obviously only the "hold dear" part is of use here.

Affection is "tender feeling or warm liking".

From there I combined both meanings. What you get is something like, "a feeling of tender and warm liking that causes one to hold something dear". Now, that awkward statement has to be pumped up, since love is not just affection but "deep" or "great" affection. So, love is, "a deep feeling of greatly tender and warm liking that causes one to strongly hold something very dear". Yes, it's now even more awkward! But that mess can be boiled down to just two words.

To strongly, tenderly and warmly hold something you deeply like and hold very dear, sounds like a description of an *embrace*. Right? And to "embrace" is to "accept willingly". So love is about ACCEPTANCE! Not a little but a great amount of acceptance. Deep, tender, warm acceptance. Perhaps it could be called "deeply embracing acceptance". I'll shorten that a bit to just, "DEEP ACCEPTANCE". That's the two words I'm boiling it all down to. Oddly enough "acceptance" is never mentioned in the dictionary definitions of love that I sampled.

To be honest I came up with "deep acceptance" long before I did the little word game. That was an experiment I hoped would somehow lead to something interesting and perhaps back up my original perception. Yes it's totally cheating, being as I clearly had a bias that influenced the results! But hey, it still could have failed miserably. That it lead to something that I could easily translate into "deep acceptance" holds some significance. Or at least it does to me.

Looking at the definition of "accept" it says, "to receive willingly or with approval". Acceptance is such a basic and fundamental part of what love is that perhaps it's too obvious to notice; hiding in plain sight. But what would love be without it? It couldn't exist.

You might disagree because sometimes a person loves someone but also rejects and disapproves of them. This might seem to prove love is something other than acceptance, but if you look closely, what's being rejected and disapproved of is their behavior or bad qualities. The love that's felt is for a deeper part of them that *is* accepted and approved of; or "received willingly". If that kernel of acceptance was not there, then neither would love be.

To be clear I should point out I'm talking about

acceptance on a *felt* level, not an *intellectual* level. Love is a feeling, not a thought. More precisely I'm saying love is a felt state/experience of deep acceptance. But I'm not saying that's all it is, just that's the essential nature or fundamental element of what love is. That is its core; which stands to reason, being as acceptance is at the core of all pleasure. Felt acceptance, pleasure and love are deeply interrelated. They are all aspects of one thing.

BYPRODUCTS

Of course there's much more to love than just acceptance. All the words I eliminated earlier still play a part.

For instance -

Because we desire, value and appreciate love, so we desire, value and appreciate what/who we love.

Because we are attracted and attached to love, so we are attracted and attached to what/who we love.

Because we are interested in and care about love, so we are interested in and care about what/who we love.

Because we are passionate about and devoted to love, so we are passionate about and devoted to what/who we love.

So most the words I earlier eliminated are brought back in as connected aspects of love. Love also inspires great kindness, fairness, empathy, and compassion, because acceptance brings us closer; just as resistance/rejection pushes us further apart. Love is about connection, closeness and union

SATISFACTION AND FULFILLMENT

The good hedonist's goal isn't just pleasure but a level of satisfaction or fulfillment where resistance has been overcome to the degree that one's wants and demands are silenced and a certain high level of acceptance is attained. It's a more complete or full state of acceptance. Since love is arguably the deepest, fullest and most complete state of acceptance, nothing brings greater satisfaction or fulfillment than love does.

The ultimate goal of the good hedonist turns out to be a certain state of love.

ROMANTIC LOVE

Our culture really pushes romantic love as the ultimate thing or experience one can have. So if you don't have it you may feel completely left out. This alienates, isolates, frustrates, invalidates and fills people with want. One can feel powerless and helpless before the glaring fact that such love can't be forced; not from others, yourself, or the Universe. Love becomes a rarefied substance hard to obtain and controlled by unseen forces. All of this causes one to resist and reject their life and the moment they are in, blocking happiness and creating despair and misery.

That's why it's so important to understand that love is not just about interpersonal relations; and "romantic love" is not necessarily the ultimate love or experience. In fact "romantic love" is sometimes just an "in love" state, which isn't so special at all.

The point I want to drive home is that love is a state of being that's available to *everyone*, even if there is no one you love or who loves you. And it's not something you have no control over. You can generate it within yourself independent of an object of that love.

Defining love as "deep acceptance" helps get that point across and free one from misconceptions that limit love to only the fortunate. Though love can't be forced, the movement toward it can be learned, because acceptance can be learned. And understanding that is liberating.

LOVE OF GOD?

Love of God can be trivialized as something akin to a delusional crush on an imaginary friend, or bullshit paraded around publicly in a self-serving, ego-driven farce. Certainly we see enough of that sort of "love" bandied about to turn our stomachs, but those aren't the only sorts of "love of God" that exist. Since I've personally experienced deeply profound and ecstatic "love of God" states myself, I know there's plenty more to the subject. And the good news is it's not just for the religious or believers of God. As a "state of being" it's available to all.

What I'm saying is that anyone, regardless of belief, can access ecstatic states which might be called "love of God". While an atheist will no doubt prefer to use other terms for it, it's still the same phenomenon. When "deep acceptance" reaches a certain crescendo it takes on qualities that are so beyond oneself it can easily be described as feeling like you are in the presence of God. It's like hitting the mother-load of love that's pouring out of the heart of existence, and it fills you to overflowing. I assure you it's not as silly as it may sound! And once experienced, a bit of it stays with you, a connection that remains. So I can understand how people feel changed by the experience; they are.

As far as I can tell, all of the grandest states of pleasure are infused with intense love. It seems to be what they are made of. How one interprets those states is up to them. Keep in mind there are many very different and often nebulous concepts of "God" - some far removed from the anthropomorphic versions that are so easy to dismiss - so "love of God" can mean lots of different things to different people.

I've had trouble getting that last point across to atheists. They tend to recognize only simple anthropomorphic creator/controller concepts of "God", and flippantly and offhandedly reject any others. It's simply much easier to maintain a stance of disbelief if you're dealing with only one narrow definition and avoiding messy or inconvenient alternatives. It's even possible to disbelieve in concepts you've never even heard of, if your model of reality is sufficiently narrow, ridged, and closed enough. Not to say that's always a bad thing, but certainty is a form of faith and is always subject to being misplaced. Understanding that brings humility to any belief; and that bit of humility is invaluable. Why? Because it is the opening that allows one to surpass their own beliefs.

TRANSCENDING PLEASURE

Acceptance is the humble path, opened to all, that begins at the slightest bit of tolerance and leads all the way up to the grand elevations of total ecstatic love-bliss. Defining love simply as "deep acceptance" doesn't really do it justice. Understand that I don't mean to limit love, but rather to provide a key to open it up and remove the impurities attached to it. Seeing its true nature as "deep acceptance" allows one to separate out all the attached desires, wants, demands, fears, hopes, dreams, expectations, and anticipations. Although acceptance is the ground love stands on, the path to its chambers, and the direction of its nature, love is also the experience and deep appreciation of the transcendent glory and joy of existence. Love is the pleasure that transcends pleasure, giving it, and everything, deeper meaning and ultimate fulfillment. Love is not a static state; it's in constant motion, both expanding outward and pulling together in living union. Love is an insight into a sublime and profound beauty that connects us all. It's what makes the price we pay in existing worthwhile; the treasure you'd gladly step out into the abyss and give your all for.

I'm sure it sounds to many like I'm going quite overboard, or nuts, in my description, but I really don't think I'm overstating it. This is my experience, and as far as I can tell, love is as deeply satisfying and fulfilling as pleasure gets, and has no limit. Thus it is the hedonist's godhead.

The good hedonist travels on the trail of acceptance, using love as a compass, because it always points the right way.

23

SEX IS OVERRATED

One might assume sex and hedonism go together like fireworks and the Fourth of July. After all, it's one of the greatest pleasures we have at our disposal. Right?

What's being ignored in that assumption is the vast amounts of suffering and discontent generated by our sex drives. Think about it. All the frustration, anxiety, craving, disappointment, dissatisfaction, resentment, embarrassment, awkwardness, manipulation, deceit, objectifying, selfishness, addiction, depression, fear, anger, regret, guilt, shame, alienation, crushed egos, blue balls, physical injuries, abuse, and crimes generated around sex. It's not a pretty picture.

Although sex certainly can be quite pleasurable, our sex drive itself is a biologically created *demand* that can cause all the same sorts of troubles, suffering and mayhem that other demands do. Suffering is built into its functioning just as much as pleasure is. Both psychological and physical discomforts are basic components of how our sex drives manipulate us. Nature wants us to breed and it wields the carrot and the stick with merciless conviction. Sex is a "temple of pleasure" with a very large torture dungeon.

But let's put all the messy issues generated by the sex drive aside and just focus on the sex act itself. How does it rate as a source of pleasure?

Well, if you ask individuals the answers would be all

over the map; from hating it, to the greatest thing in the universe. Which points out one of its flaws: Sexual pleasure varies greatly from person to person. So its value as a pleasure generator varies greatly.

What if we take just those that rate it very high, which I'd assume are the majority. Are they overrating sex?

In a word, yes. I'm not saying they aren't experiencing great pleasure, but rather that the pleasure is not all coming directly from sex. In the best sexual experiences the greatest sources of pleasure are from the emotional or "spiritual" spheres, not the sexual or sensual. It's the intense feelings of intimacy, acceptance, union, love and transcendence that reach up into ecstasy and bliss, not the physical stimulation. While the physical sensations can be very pleasant or intense and act as a trigger or catalyst leading to these greater pleasures, they alone are never ecstasy or bliss. Sex stripped of emotion or transcendent feelings is simply not such a big deal.

I'm sure some will disagree with me, especially when it comes to the physical orgasm. Of course on a subjective level they'd all be right (what's true for them is true for them) but I'm trying to judge more objectively and using a scale of quality, not quantity or intensity. A strictly physical sexual orgasm, stripped of emotional or transcendent feelings, is a spasmodic release of tension not that far removed from a sneeze. Quite involving but not really all that special. Sure, it can release a lot of tension in one very intense crescendo, which sounds pretty handy, but when you consider most of that tension is generated by the sex drive itself, it loses much of its handiness. And although it's certainly compelling and intense, which can be an attraction in itself, it doesn't rate high on the quality scale.

But of course most sexual experiences are not strictly physical and stripped of emotional or transcendent feelings, so usually something of a "big deal". The point I'm trying to make is that the best pleasures in sex are not unique to sex. They may seem uniquely special, because they are highlighted against the backdrop of intense *want* our sex drives create. It's a trick of perspective, much like how a piece of stale bread seems quite special when you're starving. The sex drive's ability to create a very similar state of "starvation" is key to how it operates. The itch that must be scratched.

The bottom line is that sex, as a source of pleasure, is a limited venue/commodity with uneven results and many practical limitations; such as you simply can't physically do it all the time, and even if you could it eventually gets boring and unpleasant. So, if sex is your greatest pleasure you'll be trapped by its many limitations and drawbacks. That's why the good hedonist must realize that the greatest pleasures sex has to offer are actually not from sex itself and are available elsewhere. Then sex doesn't become a gatekeeper between you and what you want, thus holding vast power over you with an unending ability to generate suffering. You can't be free if that's the case. And if you are free, then accessing the more sublime pleasures during sex is that much easier.

The good hedonist does not overvalue or get dependent on sex, understanding its greatest pleasures are from domains freely available elsewhere.

24

DRUGS ARE FOR THE INCOMPETENT

If one is skilled and competent at generating pleasure on their own, there is little use for any recreational drugs. It's only the poorly skilled and incompetent hedonist who must resort to drugs to create states of enjoyment. Drug use testifies to what is lacking in the user, not to a strength.

But are drugs a good idea for the unskilled and incompetent hedonist? If one finds they enjoy a certain drug, then why not use it? After all, a hedonist is supposed to be about enjoyment, right?

The obvious answer that might be given is the usual stuff we've all heard about the serious dangers and problems of drug and alcohol use and abuse. While that certainly is an issue of concern, the fact is most drug/alcohol users manage to avoid becoming addicts or ruining their lives and health. So, unless the drug in question is something exceptionally risky, like heroin or some chemical made in a shack, it's not a very convincing argument to not use any drugs recreationally at all. Much like saying one shouldn't drive because some people crash. But there is a much less recognized negative dynamic of drug use that actually affects 100% of users and is of particular concern for the aspiring good hedonist.

When you use a drug to induce pleasure you

essentially are using that drug to force a state of acceptance. But force is in opposition to acceptance, so though the act may result in some pleasure, it is also leading one in the wrong direction, creating a manipulative relationship with pleasure that can never attain the deeply fulfilling states the good hedonist seeks.

While first use of a drug can be an exploration you may learn something from, repeated recreational use is always a manipulation. None can escape that dynamic. And that's why the good hedonist must steer clear of being a regular recreational drug user. It's simply the wrong relationship to have with pleasure and there is no way to make it otherwise. If pleasure becomes a commodity that you buy with a drug, then it's reduced to something far short of the sublime miracle it truly is.

Of course, if you're fine with being an incompetent hedonist with second rate pleasure that will never get any better and most likely decline substantially, go ahead and do whatever you want. I'm certainly for people being able to do what they wish with their own bodies and minds. But the good hedonist treads a delicate path and must use great caution. Their relationship to pleasure is not something to be trifled with or taken lightly. Inserting a drug into that dynamic has consequences.

Because our drive toward pleasure and away from suffering is so fundamental and powerful, if a drug becomes too attached to that drive then it can control you through it; which is not a position anyone should want to be in.

The good hedonist doesn't let a drug become the

gatekeeper between them and pleasure.

AVOIDANCE

Using a drug to bury, avoid or try to heal unpleasant feelings is a very common tactic. Anything we find pleasure in might be used in this way. Especially things we can easily manipulate, such as drugs, food, sex, shopping, gambling, killing hobos, or whatever. But none of these actually deal with the problem, so it festers. This sort of tactic at dealing with suffering insures that no progress can be made or skill developed, and any existing skill will be weakened, thus making yourself even more vulnerable. It can also easily become an ingrained habit or addiction negatively impacting your life in major ways. While at times there is usefulness in temporary relief, if that's all you're doing, things will probably get worse. And if you're playing with fire, well, you know how that story goes.

HYSTERIA AND HYPERBOLE

Back when crack cocaine was a new sensation it was common to see news stories exclaiming, "One hit and you're hooked!" Or there would be some sort of scientist declaring, "It goes straight to the brain's pleasure center!" They kept pushing the idea that crack caused such intense enjoyment that no one could resist it. Addicts were paraded out raving, "It's better than sex!" or "It's the best experience in the world!" The onslaughts of hysterical sound bites were supposed to be warnings but they mainly served as free advertising for crack dealers. It's pretty hard to not be curious about "the best experience in the world!"

Of course it was all a load of sensationalized crap. Truth for certain addicts perhaps, but certainly not for everyone. You might try crack and hate it. Or at least not think it such a big deal. I'm living proof of that. I once smoked some crack just to prove to an addicted friend that it was not irresistible. Sure enough, I wasn't impressed in the least and have never had the slightest urge to take another hit. While I am a tough critic, my "pleasure center" actually did remain untouched. So either I'm a freak (which I may be) or the claims made were quite faulty.

There's no drug everyone enjoys. None. That simple fact proves there is no drug that actually "goes straight to the brain's pleasure center". In other words, no drug directly creates pleasure. The path is always less direct and we are always part of the process. We bring pleasure to the drug, not the other way around. We hold the power of enjoyment and should never surrender that power over to a drug, thinking it the creator of pleasure.

Which is easier said than done. If you enjoy the effects of a drug it's hard not to see it as creating that pleasure. It's a powerful illusion. But actually the drug is only producing some effects that you personally interpret as very acceptable, and it's that reaction of acceptance that produces the pleasure. The greater and deeper the acceptance, the greater and deeper the pleasure.

After that happens, the association of that drug to pleasure will be set in your mind and body, producing cravings for the drug. Indulge those cravings enough and you'll develop a level of dependence. And once dependence is established, what started as the easy route to pleasure has become an obstacle to pleasure, where every good-time or moment of relaxation must include the drug or it doesn't quite satisfy. The tool of manipulation has hijacked the person's natural ability to experience pleasure. It's a sad and pathetic state to be in, and usually the individual is unaware of it.

The essential point is this: We all have the power within us to create pleasure on our own. While in some limited instances a drug may serve to help reveal that power, relying on a drug for pleasure does the opposite, creating more and more distance between you and that power until it's lost in a far off haze.

The good hedonist is skilled and competent at producing pleasure and overcoming suffering, so recreational drugs hold little attraction or function.

PULLING YOUR OWN BOOTSTRAPS

Drugs, sex, eating, shopping, sky diving, ping pong, etc.; all have limitations, but pleasure itself does not. So the good hedonist seeks to access and expand pleasure directly from within rather than depend only on the manipulation of things in the physical world, or the whims of good fortune, to acquire pleasure. To be able to extract pleasure out of thin air, in effect pulling yourself up by your own bootstraps, is a liberation that transforms one's relationship to pleasure, and the Universe.

The good hedonist is liberated by the skills they hold within.

25

THE SHIT HOLE

The "shit-hole" is when everything looks and feels like shit. Your subjective mental picture of reality takes a nosedive to purely negative. You feel depleted, powerless, disconnected and isolated; a helpless spec of suffering trapped in a in a drab, pointless pit of despair. The world around you, or even the entire universe, appears an ugly, cold, empty abomination, echoing bleak misery from its every pore.

Okay, I laid it on pretty thick! It's not always so dramatic, but you get the point. If you don't, well maybe you're one of those lucky people who never experience anything like it. But I'd wager most do, to some degree at some time or another. So being able to deal with "The Shit Hole" is a useful skill.

Shit-hole experiences are usually short lived, but even an hour feels like an eternity. It may seem to come out of nowhere, trapping you in Shitsville with no perceived way out. Perhaps it's a relic of old damage coaxed to the surface by almost anything. A situation, a smell, a sight, a feeling, or just being rundown, whatever. There's lots rattling around inside us, and our minds can construct how "reality" feels from the refuse it finds scattered about in our skulls.

I should interject here that drug use can make major "shit-hole" experiences more likely to occur. After all, messing with your brain chemistry and mental circuits has repercussions, and "highs" can crash to abysmal lows. There can be a heavy price to pay and it's important to realize when this is the cause so you don't keep repeating it. Sadly some are willing to endure a colossal amount of suffering for their drug. (Mental shit-hole? No problem. Live in an actual shit-hole? No problem. Shit in your pants? No problem!)

The Shit-hole is all bleak ugliness, isolation, dread, despair, and suffering. There is no beauty, hope, love, or pleasure in it. Normally what we experience is a mixture of suffering and pleasure, resistance and acceptance. When both are in view it allows you to focus on increasing one and lessening the other. With only the negative in view it's hard to do anything but sit there and suffer. If all you can see is shit you can't accept, the very notion of acceptance can seem beyond your grasp.

Lost and abandoned in negativity, one needs a speck of light to show the way. A map, a sign, a direction, a clue. Without which all you can do is wait it out, which is always a viable option, since, as I said, the shit-hole is usually short lived.

What I've found helps is to recognize that the Shit-hole you are seeing and feeling around you is not a very accurate representation of reality. While no one can deny that aspects of our universe/reality truly are ugly, cold and unpleasant, they certainly aren't everything. So at best it's a very incomplete picture of reality with the shitty parts presented as all. At worst it's a complete fabrication one's mind has constructed, using your fears and anxieties as foreman on the project. Something of a personal freak show.

Bottom line is that whether it's a half-truth or complete fabrication, it's bullshit posing as truth. So don't give it much weight. It's just some crap that will pass. A half-assed or false picture of reality that ignores and excludes all that is beautiful, good, and worthwhile. It's like passing off a pile of elephant intestines as being the whole elephant. It's nonsense, because there is so much more to reality than the shit-hole. So try to not take it too seriously. It's a bad joke. Give it the finger and remind yourself of all the good that is being left out. Think of what you value. Think of someone you love. Think of the fact that rather than being an isolated, alienated, abandoned being in a bleak wasteland of despair, as the Shit-hole says, you are actually connected to everything. No matter what you are feeling, the fact is you are an intimate part of the Universe. You are accepted, connected, held, and embraced by the Universe, life, and existence itself. You couldn't exist otherwise. To be rejected by the Universe, is to not exist at all.

The Shit-hole is just an illusion where the Universe is our cold indifferent tomb, but it's actually what has given us life and is still giving us life in each moment we exist. Though we can imagine and feel separation from the cosmos, there never really is any.

The good hedonist is not taken in by their mind's bullshit.

PART 2 - THE REAL SHIT HOLE

I spent two years taking care of someone close to me that was slowly dying of cancer. This person was in a very real "shit-hole" and it was horrendous. I'm at a loss at how to deal with such. It's too viscerally real and overpowering, and I've only seen it from the outside as an observer. All I can offer here is my humility, regret and sympathy to anyone facing a real shit-hole. I can't even offer advice to those watching such happen. It's just hard, hard, hard, and no intellectual bullshit I could spew is going to help much.

The good hedonist withstands the seeming indifference of the universe by valuing and embracing it's opposite.

26

THE INDIFFERENT UNIVERSE

The physical universe appears to treat us with complete indifference, like a machine would. There was a time I thought that proved there was no God or any sort of "higher power" and I existed within a cold, mechanical universe. While it does seem to disprove the sort of God or higher power that manipulates the world whenever he/she/it feels like it, all it solidly proves is that's how the physical laws of the physical universe operate. But the Universe* is more than just the laws of physics. We conscious, experiencing, feeling beings aren't alien invaders, we are a part of the Universe just as much as anything else within it. To look at just the physical world and conclude that's solely what the Universe is, is to ignore one hell of a lot of reality. Reality that is not indifferent.

As a kid it never occurred to me that I was a part of the Universe, not an accidental anomaly trapped within its cold indifference. The physical world has such a large and imposing presence, while I was a fragile bit that appears and then soon disappears. What was I compared to it? Not much, was my conclusion. For me the physical universe was 99.99999% of reality and whatever that last .00001% was didn't matter. I was seeing the "pile of guts" as the whole elephant.

---

*When I capitalize "Universe" I'm uniting the physical universe with our inner universe and seeing them as one.

I see things differently now, but that old vision still lingers in my head, looking for a toehold to reestablish itself. It's a powerful model of reality that seduces with both its simplicity and intimidating presence. The physical universe seems so much more substantial than us tiny temporary creatures that infect this small bit of rock.

Certainly it's a hell of a lot bigger than our bodies, but how big is it compared to consciousness? How large is mental space and how much can be contained within it? How vast and varied is conscious experience? Does the physical universe have any value if we conscious beings didn't exist and find value in it?

The point is the non-physical universe is at least a worthy counterpart to the physical universe, and together they are the Universe we know. I see it as something like other dualities/polarities that are such a common aspect of reality. But however one chooses to see it, the fact remains that both parts are equally real and substantial, and together are the Universe we are part of.

Most people pick one side over the other, creating a bias which colors all they see. Materialist or Spiritual, Religious or Atheist, Realist or Dreamer, Darwinism or Creationism, PBS or Porn (Okay, that last one made no sense!). It's difficult to exist in a neutral state. Like being on the top of a greased hill, any movement will have you sliding one way or the other. That doesn't mean you're doomed to join any of the groups massed on either side. The good news is you can define things for yourself. Which, you may have noticed, I've been doing a lot of.

The physical universe is worthless without

consciousness. That isn't a bias or "subjective" point of view, it's a fact because value can't exist without consciousness and the ability to experience pleasure and suffering. So, rather than a "fragile bit" of not much consequence, we conscious beings are what gives value and meaning to the Universe, and in that way are as large and imposing as the vastness of space.

I know that sounds like a big ego trip! I guess it could be for some, but I mean this to go quite beyond our individual egos. It's consciousness and the full spectrum of experience it makes possible that is the crucible of value, not our individual egos and personalities. We serve it, not the other way around. All experiences in the upper reaches of pleasure inspire true humility, because our true position becomes obvious.

The "indifferent universe" is the ground we walk on, not the full measure of reality. Pleasure and suffering are the antithesis of indifference.

The good hedonist sees that everything serves that which gives value to all.

27

RELIGION IS ABOUT PLEASURE
WHETHER THEY LIKE IT OR NOT

Religions tend to downplay or even denigrate pleasure, yet that really is all they are about. After all, what good is a religion if it doesn't ultimately offer more pleasure and less suffering? What would be the point? But they usually are in denial about it, preferring to believe they're about something more respectable or noble than pleasure.

Such a schizophrenic condition is unhealthy, creating deep inner conflicts and problems. Self-hate and/or the hatred of others are a grave danger in such a divided state. And to shore up their unstable model of reality and avoid their true selves, they are driven to create beliefs of evil forces or their own superiority and specialness. Elaborate schemes to avoid a simple truth that doesn't need to be avoided in the first place.

People often fail to recognize that pleasure is just as linked to our very highest and noblest drives as it is our very lowest and crudest urges. Our higher nature is just as much about pleasure as our lower one is. It's just more sophisticated, having discovered greater pleasures that are more beautiful, profound, satisfying and fulfilling. When religion helps us discover those greater pleasures it serves a good purpose. When it alienates us from our true selves and creates divisions between people, it serves us poorly.

GOD TOLD ME YOU SUCK

The most unfortunate thing about religion is when it acts as a force of division. That can happen in subtle ways or in outright open bigotry sanctified in scriptures and doctrines. When God is seen as dividing humanity between believers and non-believers, issuing reward to one and condemnation or punishment to the other, it acts as a veritable bigotry machine pumping out its sanctified poison without regard; a corrupting acid eating away at the congregation*. Only religions that don't divide believer and non-believer, seeing them as equal in both their eyes and God's, avoid this tragic negative undercurrent.

The good hedonist makes no distinction between believers and non-believers, because he/she knows we all are just simply hedonists.

REALITY NAILED DOWN - NOT!

Each religion has its own model of reality. It's very important to recognize that true reality can never be contained in a model, a thought, or nailed down by words. It simply cannot fit into your skull. So all models of reality, be they from religion, science, or whatever, are to a degree false. So everyone should have a healthy amount of humility and not become too proud or sure in their beliefs.

---

*Of course bigotry flows both ways. Smug non-believers that think they are superior to the religious can be just as bigoted, dividing and poisonous.

Ultimate truth, ultimate reality is where we live and what we are. It is ours. Our truth. Our reality. We are completely one with it but it can't be fully understood with our mind through thoughts. It's through felt experience that we come closest to it, and closest to understanding the mystery. That is the direct path: The way that touches the thing itself. All other methods are abstractions; words and symbols, thoughts and concepts that can never fully encircle reality. Only our embrace can wrap around it.

The good hedonist's focus on felt experience may be the greatest tool for discovering ultimate truth, for it is by experience only that we can touch the "divine".

IN AND OUT OF GRACE

The religious often mistake the benefits of acceptance as proof of the veracity of their religion and God. Believing "God is in control", or that you are in the graces of the true divine religion sanctioned by the most high, can inspire great acceptance and letting go of one's demands. The peace and good feelings that naturally follow are attributed to their God and religion because they don't understand the basic dynamics of how states of acceptance can affect them, or how suffering and pleasure are generated.

A danger of this sort of thinking is that when things aren't going so well one might conclude that something evil is afoot, or you are out of God's graces in some way. After all, if you believe you clearly had a sign of God's grace and that grace leaves you, what do you blame? It's natural to look for an answer, but the conclusions one might come to within certain religious belief systems can be pretty damn scary. This can cause great paranoia, anxiety, confusion, depression and suffering.

While the good hedonist sees pleasure also as a grace, that grace is never earned, rewarded, given or taken away. Grace is simply the nature of pleasure itself.

GOD IS LOVE?

Hedonism is most in line with religions that declare "God is Love", because love is in the good hedonist's holy of holies. As I said in the chapter on love, "Love is the pleasure than transcends pleasure, giving it, and everything, deeper meaning and ultimate fulfillment."

Unfortunately, no religion I know of keeps it that simple. They always have to ruin it with much added detail.

The good hedonist isn't anti-spiritual or materialistic; he/she doesn't divide reality in such a way. "Spirit" and matter are always one.

28

MATERIALIST FUNDAMENTALISM

Just as a religious fundamentalist takes the scriptures of their religion and interprets them in a very literal, dogmatic, simplistic, and inflexible way, the materialist fundamentalist does the same with science. Though they think they are being very rational and only facing the facts, they neglect to consider the limitations of what science reveals about reality, or notice the degree to which they've filled in the unknown with their own mythology and unproven assumptions. They apply reductionism to construct their imagined world. Life is reduced to certain amino acids randomly coming together. The meaning of our existence is reduced to the survival of DNA. Love is reduced to chemicals. Consciousness reduced to neural structures. Everything boiled down to just the physical bits we know, denying anything beyond that doesn't fit into their neat little model.

This has deeply negative implications, as it misrepresents pleasure, love, consciousness, reality and our position within the universe to such an extreme degree. Rather than embracing the grand mystery of these things, they place them on the shelf of known items, next to the beakers of chemicals and jars of tissue samples. Blind to how inadequate and ridiculous that is, they lean back satisfied.

Science is a wonderful thing that has expanded humanities knowledge to unimaginable heights. The scope of what it's achieved really is mind blowing and inspires great faith in its capabilities. This can make it difficult to see its limitations and weaknesses; or to understand that it, like religion, can create in us an illusion that we know more than we actually do. Not to imply it's the fault of science, but rather a fault of our own ignorance, emotions, and psychological frailties.

It's fairly easy for someone to assume that because we know E=mc2 that means we know what energy is; but no one really does. The limits of what scientific facts say are often the hardest part to grasp. Especially for us lay people, because it often takes a more in-depth and nuanced state of knowledge to really understand. Few have the time or energy for that. Most of us just want to know enough to form a comfortable feeling. So we take shortcuts, make assumptions, ignore, gloss over and develop biases.

A materialist fundamentalist can write off something as deeply mysterious as consciousness to merely something evolution crapped out and not give it a second thought. Sure, evolution explains a lot but let's not go nuts and think it's a legitimate answer for nearly everything. Don't use it like religious fundamentalists use God, as an easy catch-all explanation cementing up areas you don't wish to contemplate. Don't let it be an expression of a lazy, inflexible, arrogant, frightened, or in-denial mind unwilling to face or accept the profound mystery that is such a fundamental part of our reality and being.

Here we sit, a miracle within a miracle. Springing forth from a Universe at whose very core are laws of physics so mind blowing that no one fully understands them or how they came to be. Both we and the Universe are an ineffable mystery and anyone telling you differently is a fool.

Whatever anyone can explain there is always something just beyond it that's unexplained. Wherever you make a line in the sand there's always space beyond. You'll never find an end to it. At some point everyone must throw up their hands and concede they have no clue.

The Universe is always, at its fundamental heart, a profoundly unaccountable marvel. It may make you feel good to believe you're one of the smart, learned, rational, brave, blessed, lucky or superior people that knows what's really going on, but that's only an illusion you've created in your mind to avoid discomfort and fear of the unknown. Your model of reality serves as the line in the sand you refuse to venture beyond. That line limits your reality to a size and form you can comfortably fit within your skull. It's the border of your imagined world. And like in ancient maps, it has an edge where you can fall off. It's the edge of your understanding, where God and the Big Bang roam like the great sea monsters of old, policing the boarder. It takes some real guts to enter the unknown waters, but that is the realm where we actually abide: Our real home. Go on, dare to step out there.

The good hedonist must travel beyond their model of reality, because that's where the greatest pleasures lie.

29

THE GROUND OF REALITY

If you know anything about quantum physics, you know it's profoundly weird and difficult to understand. Actually, it's not just difficult to understand, no one fully understands it. No one. Don't let anyone fool you into thinking they do. The more anyone knows about it the more they know how truly unfathomable it is.

The deeper we look into the quantum world, the more it flees from our sight, retreating into an impenetrable mist. It's a pursuit that could very well go on forever, but it's hard to not feel that we will someday catch up to it and finally understand what is at the core of our physical reality. After all, we've solved a million other mysteries, why not this one?

Well, it may just be an impossible task, like trying to nail down the wind. Efforts to prove what photons are only deepened the mystery with experiments that simultaneously proved they are particles and proved they are waves. So what are they? No one really knows. We only know how they behave in certain situations. Sometimes like a particle, sometimes like a wave. The photon's true nature is an enigma and will probably always stay that way; same as the entire quantum world. We will no doubt learn more about it, but, as so often is the case, that will most likely just expose even greater mysteries about its true nature.

The thing that draws us to science or religion is our

desire to feel we understand. Which isn't a bad inclination, unless we get smug in it. There should always be a base of humility, because no matter how much knowledge we may acquire, in truth we are all sitting deeply within a colossal mystery our minds can't fully grasp. That is our reality. Losing sight of it creates a barrier, a self-contained false image of reality that separates us from a vital and fundamental element of our truth. We bounce around inside self-manufactured echo chambers seeing only the walls we have created. But when one has the humility to accept that they really don't know what reality actually is, then the chamber opens and the echo is set free to explore the limitless horizon. What was limited becomes unlimited.

The good hedonist never encases the Universe within his/her mind.

30

OBJECTIVE VS SUBJECTIVE

There's a bias against what might be called "subjective" reality, the realm of our consciousness, mind and experience. For some it's seen as a sort of secondary artifact that's less *real* than "objective" reality, the physical world. Such a division can't be good since it places such a vital and intimate part of ourselves in a lower standing than, say, a rock.

A strict materialist sees consciousness as merely an anomaly farted out by evolutionary happenstance, existing solely to help perpetuate one's DNA. To them our inner world is an illusion seen by a phantom that's created by our physical parts and processes. No matter how wonderful they may think consciousness is, to them it will always be a second-hand artifact sprouting off from physical reality.

It's not hard to see how this bias came about. After all, the physical universe existed long before any conscious creatures. That would seem to say consciousness is a secondary artifact that somehow sprang from the physical world. The only kink in that reasoning is there's no way to tell when or where consciousness itself actually began. Was it at the first brain? First nervous system? First one celled organism? First living thing? Or is it something more fundamental that exists in some minor way on even an atomic or subatomic level? When a particle reacts to an outside force, could you call that "awareness"? Is that an elementary form of consciousness? Where do you draw the line with certainty? Could consciousness be a fundamental quality of the universe, like space/time, gravity, mass, or energy? Who the hell can say? There's simply no way to prove or disprove it, so whichever way you believe, it's a matter of faith or self-delusion.

To me it would make much more sense if life and evolution built upon a fundamental quality that already existed in the universe, rather than just farting consciousness out by happenstance. As a conscious being myself, I certainly don't feel like a fart of happenstance! A mere ghostlike aftereffect sprouting from something more "real" and substantial through some mechanical evolutionary process that somehow blindly shit out a miracle. I feel as basic and primal to reality as anything in the universe. For what that's worth. And with the very substance of physical reality being so elusive, mysterious and unfathomable, I feel the elusive, mysterious and unfathomable nature of consciousness is right on par with it. "Subjective" reality appears no less real or substantial than "objective" reality.

Please understand I don't claim to know the truth of this matter. No one does, so it's a matter of faith whichever way you choose to see it. Since we are conscious beings, I think it serves us best to give consciousness and "subjective reality" the benefit of the doubt. Belief isn't necessary, only abiding openness to the possibility.

The good hedonist sees consciousness and pleasure as just as real and substantial as the physical universe.

31

THE MOST IMPORTANT THING IN THE UNIVERSE

It's my contention that the outer, objective, physical universe has no point without the inner, conscious, feeling, experiencing, subjective universe. And neither has any point without the experience of pleasure. So, it follows that pleasure is the most important thing in the Universe.

To me this seems obvious, but I have to assume that many will disagree. And there's always the possibility that I'm an idiot missing something even more obvious. So please do try to prove me wrong and come up with something else.

One might get tricky and say consciousness itself was more important, since without it pleasure couldn't exist. But what good is consciousness without pleasure? If you can't ever enjoy anything, why be conscious?

Love? Well, love is a pleasure, perhaps the chief pleasure, so it's not only included in my statement but crowns it.

Enlightenment? What good is that if it doesn't lead to more pleasure and less suffering? If the state of being enlightened was unpleasant would anyone want enlightenment? Well, some still might, out of curiosity at least, but would they want to stay enlightened?

Knowledge? Same answer as for enlightenment applies.

God? What is God if there is no pleasure? What would motivate God to do anything, create anything? God's love and love of God couldn't exist. And what good would heaven be if there was no love, joy or pleasure there? You might think "It would still be better than suffering in Hell!" but there is a major problem with that logic. Pleasure and suffering define one another and are poles of one thing. You can't eliminate one without the other going too, just like you can't have a north pole without a south pole. If the Universe had no possibility for pleasure there would also be no possibility for suffering. Furthermore, without pleasure and pain there would be no way to care about anything. Burning to death or lying on silk sheets would be the same. Nothing pleasant, nothing unpleasant. No preferring one thing over another. No desire could exist. No love, beauty, kindness, compassion or joy. Even values, morals, virtue, meaning and purpose would be impossible. Pleasure/suffering is the scale we use to weigh all those things. How can you decide one thing is better than another if there is no way to care? Coin flips are all you could do because all would be the same. You couldn't even feel interest in anything! Living or dying wouldn't matter. The universe would be a completely flavorless and bland, though none could feel those things.

It's sort of like the old saying, "If a tree fell in the forest…" - If a universe happened and there was nothing with the ability to appreciate it, would it have any value? Being as value and appreciation are impossible without the ability to feel pleasure and pain, a universe without pleasure would have to be of no value whatsoever.

The good hedonist knows that all meaning and value depend on the existence of pleasure.

32

WAY, WAY OUT

We depend on our models of reality to create a level of acceptance and security. It can be very unsettling to venture out beyond them, but reality is always beyond our models, completely untamed, wild, and free. A profound mystery we can never mentally unravel.

With that as the true reality we live in, and are ourselves, finding acceptance for it would be to one's advantage. That's not an easy task, being as it's so beyond our comprehension. However, the good hedonist achieves this by way of discovering the profound pleasure that resides within it.

Through the experience of pleasure we can step out into the mystery and bridge the gap our minds cannot. Pleasure is the way to find value, and thus acceptance, in something existing beyond our mental grasp. Only through pleasure can we fully embrace reality.

Acceptance and resistance are actions within that affect how we experience the Universe. Having some control over those actions, to any degree, is a source of personal power. In exercising that power you'll find how flexible and mutable our perceived world is. And also how fertile and rich it is, generating pleasure from unforeseen angles and places, sprouting beauty and joy from what once may have seemed barren ground. Reality becoming richer, fuller and of more value in an ever expanding wave. That wave engulfs everything.

Please don't get the impression this is something achieved by reaching directly for it. It's the small steps which lead there, not the large ones. The large ones are too full of desire and manifest from one's resistance. The small steps are every tiny bit of acceptance humbly mustered. They lead in the right direction. It's the very nature of acceptance to expand and unify, so the path of acceptance always flows toward the source.

The good hedonist expands acceptance beyond the boundary of their understanding.

33

MYTHS AND FALLACIES TO AVOID

There are various popular myths and fallacies that a good hedonist would be better off avoiding.

KARMA

Karma is a very popular concept which takes various forms. The standard simple dictionary definition is - "action seen as bringing upon oneself inevitable results, either in this life or in a reincarnation". It's a concept of moral causation or cause and effect. People seem to believe in this not because of any proof, reason, or logic, but because their notion of a just Universe, or God, needs karma to exist. It's simply a comfort for them to believe in it.

Often it's claimed to be like the physical law of motion where every action has an equal and opposite reaction (Newton's third law of motion). While the comparison does get their point across well, the fact is the laws of physics are backed up with real science and proof, and karma is backed up by only wishful thinking. They can try as hard as they want to associate it with science, calling karma the natural "law" of cause and effect, but there's simply nothing backing it up, and lots to question.

Karma was probably originally invented to get people to behave better; a simple reward and punishment scheme. And because it's fairly easy to see that karmic theory doesn't always jive well with the reality seen around us, reincarnation was needed to shore up that flaw; effectively making it impossible to disprove, since the proof might be well beyond our reach in other lifetimes.

It's a mechanistic model that, though ancient, even to this modern day has a wide appeal. But it's bullshit. While certainly our actions do cause reactions, those reactions do not seem to follow the karmic model with any sort of regularity. But with supposed reincarnation allowing the causes and reactions to happen in different lifetimes, all I can offer is logic and reason as proof. Just think the details through for yourself. How right would it feel to you if someone was reborn as a very different person yet had to suffer for crimes of a previous life they have no knowledge of? Does that seem just or good? Wouldn't that new incarnation be damaged by it, causing even more negative effects and actions that would generate more bad karma? Wouldn't it be a self-perpetuating circus of cruelty that could never end? Doesn't that very system sound like bad karma? And what's the karmic reaction for a bad karma karmic system?

Many claim it operates like gravity with no moral bearing whatsoever, just dealing with positive and negative "energies". But how would it determine a "positive" energy from a "negative" energy if it can't make moral value judgments? How would it tell child abuse from needed discipline, prison from kidnapping, or a boxing match from an assault?

It just gets ridiculous. What's the karmic reaction if a rapist rapes someone who was a rapist in a previous life? Or what about a father who abuses his kids and that abuse gets handed down generation after generation: Would they all be reborn to more abuse in reaction to the abuse they handed out? When would it end? Could it keep fanning out, causing more and more negative effects over the centuries, continuously piling up negative karma until humanity finally dies out? Would that original father end up with billions of lifetimes of bad karma?!

And in this modern world where we are all so connected, it's easy for one action to reverberate out to millions immediately, not just over generations. Just think how crazily complicated all that karma would get!

I certainly don't see it working in the real world. Good people get screwed over and bad people get rewarded all the time. Rarely do I see anyone get what they deserve. Lend a friend money and you are more likely to lose that friend than get any sort of good karma from it. It's just the actions of human nature: guilt, insecurity, jealousy, shame, greed, etc. Plus the fact is that good people are simply easier to take advantage of than not so good people.

When we suffer or are rewarded for past actions it isn't due to karma, it's due to the memories of us living beings and our natural reactions and proclivities. There are no score cards in the sky. No karmic memory bank. The universe doesn't store our actions for later reactions. Only we do, in our minds, hearts, and records. There's no karmic caretaker, it's up to us to reward good actions or punish bad ones. "Karma" is our responsibility to dish out. To shirk that responsibility, deferring it over to an imagined "law of karma", is a tragic mistake that leads to thinking of victims as just reaping the fruits of their own past karma; which leads to less compassion, less charity, less justice, and less action. Believing in karma can have serious negative consequences.

Concepts of karma try to manipulate behavior through appeals to our selfish nature and fears. That might trick some to behave better, but it doesn't produce better people. The things that produce better people are the abilities to experience empathy, compassion and love. These are embraced on the good hedonist's path as the natural progression of acceptance and the direction of more sublime and fulfilling pleasures. The path forward is always one of increased union and love.

Laws of karma don't exist, but laws of pleasure and suffering do. They are the compass that ultimately points us in the right direction, if we have the eyes to see.

The good hedonist has no need for laws of karma, because he/she already sees that good behavior is in his/her best interest, leading to the greatest pleasure, happiness and fulfillment.

The good hedonist knows that justice is not met out on high, but is the responsibility of each of us.

LAW OF ATTRACTION

How would you like to be able to manifest whatever

you want into your life? Sound good? Of course it does! Who could resist such god-like power?! It's very seductive stuff, and that is exactly what the so-called "Law of Attraction" promises. Sometimes it's called other things, such as "Power of Intention" or "The Secret", but it's all basically the same thing and has been around in some form or another since the early 1900's. Usually packaged and marketed as something spiritual or even scientific, but it's neither. It caters to our desires and wish to control, offering a seemingly easy solution to our frustration and disappointments in life, with no apparent downside. But there actually is a very serious downside, besides the fact it doesn't work.

The LOA theory basically says one can manipulate the Universe with their thoughts and intentions, if done correctly. In one method you form a clear idea of what you want; project that idea out into the Universe; believe, feel, and behave as if it is being given; and be open to receive it. The last two bits basically mean you shouldn't be in a state of wanting or having any negative thoughts, doubts or fears that, in this theory, would assure you didn't get what you wanted. It's sometimes put as, "ask, believe, receive".

On the surface this seems harmless enough, but since the theory also says that your negative thoughts bring negative things into your life, it's clearly not. Follow the implications of that concept to its extreme and the individual can be blamed for all the bad things that come into their life. Sickness, rape, accidents, poverty, pimples, a shopping cart with a bum wheel, you name it. Though believers in LOA often deny this, there is no way to limit the concept so it doesn't enter into this ugly area. They want it to be all positive, feel-good and nice, but it just isn't so. You can't have fire without something getting burned. I've even seen some fanatical believers blame natural disasters on the victims.

While the "law" of karma also has a negative undertow of blaming victims, it's somewhat less insidious than LOA because to falsely think you are suffering for something you did in the past, perhaps even in a previous life, is not as destructive to the individual as to falsely think your own thoughts are screwing up your life right now. That could drive you insane!

Proving LOA true or false is a bit tricky. Simply trying it out and seeing if it works is hampered by the fact that just by pure chance it's bound to sometimes appear to work. And when it fails, the purity of your thoughts or intentions could simply be blamed. One negative desire, doubt or bit of fear might be enough to gum up the works. It's rather difficult, if not impossible, to not have any of those things lurking about in you to some degree. Especially when you are someone just testing the method for the first time. How does one accomplish the "believe" part of "ask, believe, receive" before it's been shown to work? You'd have to be one hell of a gullible shmuck, or be very good at fooling yourself! For many that would be an insurmountable obstacle.

Turns out the best way to test LOA is to look into your past for evidence. That way you don't have to try to force yourself to believe, you just look for times you already naturally fulfilled, or broke, all of the LOA criteria. Don't just look for positive evidence; it's the evidence it didn't work that's the better proof. That's because positive results can always be written off as coincidence, but a "law" can't fail by coincidence. An actual law of the Universe shouldn't ever fail.

Unfortunately the propagators of the theory provide a big loophole. They never claim it will work every time, not even if you do it perfectly, because we are only "co-creators" with God or the Universe, which limits our power to manipulate the "law". The Universe, or God, can always override us. So even if you discover it failed to work every time, it's still impossible to absolutely prove it false. That loophole will always rescue it, and perhaps drive you nuts thinking the Universe or God is thwarting you at every turn! But I think a reasonable person doesn't need absolute proof. Reasonable proof will do.

So, find times you were completely positive, believing, clear about what you wanted yet not in a state of want, believing it was in hand, and open to receiving what that was with no negative resistance - but had it fail miserably. Or times you were completely negative, doubting, and closed about something yet it came out great. How often did either of those happen? Speaking for myself from the evidence in my life and those around me, there is no way I can believe in the Law of Attraction. I see no real positive correlation. Exceptions actually seem more the rule! So either the Universe or God is really messing with me and those I know, or LOA is utter bullshit.

Just look at hypochondriacs. They are filled with fear and negative thoughts, projecting out into the universe a perfect LOA recipe for attracting or manifesting disease into their life. But do they get sick any more than the rest of us? While I have no study to prove it, from what I can gather they don't. After all, shouldn't Woody

Allen have died long ago?!

Trying to manifest the reality you want through mind games is not just a waste of time, it also distracts you from appreciating the reality you are in. It's a control trip, attempting to bend the Universe to your will. A mindset of acquiring, where happiness is achieved through "manifesting" your desires. This has the unfortunate effect of leading one astray from embracing what they have in the present moment, which is the more direct and sure path to happiness.

The underlying message of the Law of Attraction is that the way to happiness is through meeting your desires: Which is no more evolved, spiritual, profound or wise than a Wall Street ad for a car or toothpaste.

Our billions of unmet desires generate a vast ocean of suffering. Much of it easily remedied by simply accepting the substantial limits of our control and the fact that we will not always get what we want. Of course the idea that we can simply manifest everything we desire is much more seductive, but it's a siren's song, leading one out onto the rocks. The good news is that happiness doesn't depend on fulfilling desires but rather on appreciating what you have right in front of you in this moment.

The good hedonist doesn't try to control the Universe, they simply enjoy it.

PROSPERITY GOSPEL

It's very common with TV preachers. They push that if you believe in God, "he" will give you prosperity in one fashion or another. They have God pulling strings in the lives of believers, granting wishes and favors simply because their faith is so strong. They'll even give credit to God for things like miraculously surviving a deadly plane crash. Never mind all the other people who died in the plane crash, or in other disasters. I guess they were all non-believers or had insufficient faith! It's truly disgusting. The arrogance to believe you are chosen over others. For what, being an idiot? Stupid, arrogant, self-absorbed nonsense. Shallow religion for shallow people: No deeper than Santa Claus. In fact it's quite a bit less deep, because Santa deals with actual good and bad behavior, not faith in some dogma. Prosperity gospel is selling wish fulfillment and self-aggrandizement, while promoting bigotry with its ugly division of the deserving faithful from the rest of humanity.

The good hedonist doesn't believe the Universe, or God, plays favorites.

FOLLOW YOUR BLISS

Following your bliss may have worked out well for Joseph Campbell but for every one of him I'll bet there are hundreds who had their "bliss" take a big dump on their heads. Besides that, "follow your bliss" can be taken as "chase after what you think will bring you happiness, even if it seems impractical or risky", which is not a good idea at all. Of course that's not what Campbell had in mind, but even if you are following what is actually giving you "bliss", rather than just chasing a desire, there are no guaranties it will pay off in any way more than the pleasure you already get out of that activity. The implication of the slogan is that somehow the Universe will embrace and reward your efforts; or as Campbell himself put it, "open doors". I'm sorry to report that is not the case. The Universe has its own agenda and it won't alter because you decide to follow your bliss. Whatever route you take, whether it's a practical course or a heartfelt one, may or may not work out. There are no guaranties. Personally, speaking as someone who followed their bliss more than most, I truly wish I'd have taken a more practical course.

While a good hedonist is following bliss, that is very different than "following *your* bliss".

YOU MUST LOVE YOURSELF BEFORE YOU CAN LOVE OTHERS

Total bullshit. I've done what this says one can't do, so without a doubt it's false: Which is lucky for us because otherwise there would be very little love in the world! Not just because few love themselves, but of those that think they do, most are just loving an idea/image of themselves that only exists in their head. That's not loving your *self*, it's loving your *ego*.

I suspect that "You must love others to love yourself" is probably more true.

WHAT DOESN'T KILL YOU ONLY MAKES YOU STRONGER

There's a grain of truth in this, as we can learn from

experience and get "stronger" in that way, and also build muscle tissue and get stronger physically. But that's not a given! What "doesn't kill you" may simply grind you down and leave you in a damaged and weakened state you may never recover from. Fanciful slogans won't help when that's the case. Let's change it to, "What doesn't kill you might possibly in certain circumstances make you stronger to some unknown degree." Catchy!

LIVE EVERY DAY AS IF IT WERE YOUR LAST

To actually do what this motto suggests would be quite impractical and exhausting: A simple recipe to ruin your life. Taken literally this could only appeal to irresponsible fools, probably with some sort of drug or alcohol problem. Nonstop party people. Or perhaps the action/adrenalin addicted. But what's often meant by this line is that one should take the time to appreciate and enjoy what they have now, rather than spend all their time striving toward a future they imagine; which is a nice sentiment. Too bad it's buried in this turd of bad advice. What's wrong with "Take the time to smell the roses"? Not "extreme" enough for you?!

ENJOY LIFE TO THE FULLEST or MAKE EVERY MOMENT COUNT

These slogans sound like demands. We don't need that sort of pressure! Besides, both would quickly become exhausting.

ONE SHOULDN'T JUDGE OTHERS

This statement is itself a judgment of others! So anyone saying it is automatically a hypocrite. But there is a baby in this bathwater, being as the word "judge" can mean several things; from simply forming an opinion, to the eternal condemnation of someone. Discerning and forming valid opinions and fair judgments is obviously good. Doing a lot of condemning of others is not so good.

NICE GUYS FINISH LAST

That was a motto of some friends I once knew. They used it as an excuse to do whatever they felt like doing. Lie, cheat and steal. Mostly steal. They considered me a "nice guy" who had morals, thus foolish and impractical. And I must admit, with them I certainly did finish last! But it could have been much worse. They were nicer than they pretended.

People with low morals take advantage of everyone, and it's the "nice" people that are trusting and/or generous who are the easiest marks. So it might seem the nice people will actually finish last. But the finish line isn't who grabs the most stuff - it's who is the most happy and fulfilled. All the ill will generated by the not so nice makes it hard for them to ever be completely happy or fulfilled. The nice have a much better chance.

Being "nice" is really about having compassion. Those who are lacking in that quality might see having it as a detriment. While it does have certain drawbacks, mainly in that it can cause us suffering, it also generates pleasure. This pleasurable side of compassion is completely overlooked, even in the definition of the word. The focus is always on compassion as being sympathy for the suffering of others, but if you can sympathize with another, then you have the ability to not just care about their suffering but also about their pleasure and joy. Which means you can take pleasure in their pleasure. Caring about others allows you to enjoy them immensely more than if you don't. It's a very important channel to a multitude of pleasures. Even our enjoyment of cute little kittens and puppies is about compassion.

The good hedonist sees that compassion is the source of many sublime pleasures.

PURITY

There's a concept in some religions and spiritual teachings that one can become more "pure" or purified. Much like the idea one can be more holy or sanctified. It's all non-sense. One can have "purer" motives, intentions or morals, but a person is always, at their core, purely what they have always been. And that can't be corrupted or soiled any more than gravity can.

THE WORD OF GOD

One could say the cosmos is the "word of God". That's the sort of speech worthy of the distinction. Our human languages are extremely pathetic in comparison: imperfect, messy, and very limited. The idea that God would communicate in human words is like Shakespeare communicating his works by throwing his turds.

Believing the words of men to be from God is a dangerous conceit that can lead to all sorts of unpleasantness.

INTELIGENT DESIGN

I truly wish we were intelligently designed; then I wouldn't have to deal with a jaw too small for my wisdom teeth. And if my physical flaws were designed on purpose, then I'd be very pissed at the sadistic designer.

This theory degrades the concept of God, in service to believing ancient scripture is the Word of God and completely factual. This mainly serves the believer's conceit, prejudices, or power games.

If your faith in God depends on scripture being 100% factual, you're vulnerable to that flaw. It's a flaw that comes from the conceit that you were 100% correct when you decided such. Such sureness is often misperceived as faith but it's really only arrogance. Humble believers avoid such blunders, and thus are less likely to suffer a devastating loss of faith (or to be colossal douche bags).

GRAND CONSPIRACY THEORIES

Some people seem to have a psychological need to believe in grand conspiracy theories, no matter how ridiculous or complicated. I've heard it said they do this out of a need to make sense of our chaotic world; which is funny, being as their theories usually make little rational sense. Still, it does simplify things to see an evil cabal behind nearly everything you don't like (much like believing in Satan), rather than a chaotic mess with such random happenstance. But we are complicated creatures and no doubt there's more behind it than just one thing. Perhaps a need to feel superior could play a part. It's a big ego blast to think you know more than the common rubes. So if the common folk believe the story in the mass media, you'll believe the story in the "alternative" media. Not because it's better researched, less biased or more logical, but because it's different. It's a kind of snobbery, a way to separate and elevate oneself. It creates three classes of people: the evil conspirators, the common naive rubes, and the more savvy folks in the know. I think this is an unhealthy way to prop up one's ego and self-esteem, functioning as a form of bigotry. To see yourself as superior, someone needs to be inferior.

One thing very noticeable in grand conspiracy believers is a strong bias of some sort, such as the bias against Jews which has excreted some of the more grotesque, vile, and long lived conspiracy theories. Negative biases help one to believe things without much questioning. They may see themselves as very "questioning", but all they're really doing is collecting questions that appear to support their bias.

One of the more popular current biases is against the United States government, or those who are seen as secretly controlling it. While it's easy to see how this can spread in other parts of the world, it's a more curious thing that it's so popular here the U.S.A. While we all have reasons to be unhappy with our government in some fashion, it's a bit strange that so many seem bent on seeing it as downright evil. Why would one prefer to see their own government behind something as wicked as 9/11, rather than the obvious and admitted perpetrators? Is it because it's more shocking? More dramatic? More devious? More complicated? More frightening? Or maybe just because it's more exciting? Might some be choosing their reality in much the same way they choose their movies? Or is it more about their fears directing their choice, like a kid who believes a monster is under their bed?

There are so many things that could be a behind it; even a subconscious desire for power, which would want our present power structure out of the way. Or simply because they are already mad at the government for whatever, and so enjoy anything which defames it. However it may be generated, there's clearly a strong bias that wants to see our government as not just incompetent, self-serving, corrupted, or jackasses, but as Satan incarnate. That can't be healthy.

Of course they aren't aware of the bias. They think they are just being rational and moved only by "facts". What they can't see is how their bias is directing which "facts" they search for and accept, and which they reject or ignore. This is often called "confirmation bias". It's not a rational process, but an emotional one. Unfortunately it's leading them to a less accurate and less pleasant version of reality.

Grand conspiracy believers, like religious fanatics, can't question their core belief. Their world model is set and to question it would require a fundamental reordering of their truth. That's very hard to do. It's much easier to simply see others as being naive, deluded, wrong, or part of the conspiracy.

The path of the good hedonist requires finding the humility to question oneself often. So it's incompatible with fanatical beliefs and mindsets. Plus anything that breeds completely unnecessary fear and hate of an evil that's not really there is detrimental to one's enjoyment of life. And you might blow your retirement savings on a cache of weapons and dehydrated food! Life is difficult enough without adding any new layers of stress. No one needs that.

The good hedonist knows that the grander the conspiracy, the less likely it's true.

34

THE ACCEPTANCE SPECTRUM

There is a spectrum to acceptance. It begins at the slightest bit of tolerance, and ends in total ecstatic bliss. Below I tried to make a list of the progression. Order may vary.

Tolerating - small amount of acceptance mixed with resistance

Resignation - grudgingly ceasing most resistance

Surrender - giving up, handing over power or control

Letting go - ceasing resistance

Allowing - non-interference, allowing moment to be as it is

Acceptance - majority acceptance over resistance

Contentment - satisfying level of acceptance

Appreciation - recognition of great value

Sacrifice - laying aside oneself in appreciation of greater value

Embracing - full acceptance, gladly taking up what is given

Gratefulness - deep appreciation of value

Happiness - overwhelming level of acceptance

Joy - exuberant savor and celebration of existence

Love - deep acceptance, union, grace

Bliss - complete harmony, cup flows over

Fulfillment - complete satisfaction, all desire extinguished

If this sounds like a recipe to become a mushy ball of peaceful protoplasm, please understand this isn't about outward behavior, it's just a list of the various flavors and expressions that acceptance can have within oneself in the movement away from suffering and toward greater pleasure.

The good hedonist does not discriminate between levels of acceptance, finding great value in each.

35

PLEASURE IS A GRACE

When one's relationship to pleasure is formulaic, manipulative, or controlling, the quality of the pleasure suffers. The skilled hedonist must have a deep respect and reverence for pleasure itself, because pleasure is an art and a grace, not merely a physical condition to be manipulated.

Though we make our many efforts, it always feels like luck and grace when one enters the upper realms of pleasure. Bliss is never bought, never earned, never harnessed, always free. It's a glorious masterpiece, art flowering as life beheld. A grace that transcends all, and the good hedonist stands humbled before it.

For the good hedonist, pleasure is a grace and should always be greeted as such with humility, for it can't be fully appreciated otherwise.

36

SUMMARY

From resisting to accepting

From rejecting to embracing

From separation to union

That is the direction of the good hedonist

www.ingramcontent.com/pod-product-compliance
Lightning Source LLC
Chambersburg PA
CBHW060926040426
42445CB00011B/809